M000192410

DE LONG'S
WINE GRAPE
VARIETAL
TABLE

SECOND EDITION

WINE AND GRAPE
INDEXES

to Leo

DE LONG'S WINE GRAPE VARIETAL TABLE
SECOND EDITION

First Edition Published 2002

PRINTED IN THE UNITED STATES OF AMERICA

ISBN 0-9723632-1-1

Visit our website at www.delongwine.com

NOTES ON THE SECOND EDITION

We would like to thank the many people who gave us comments and criticism on the first edition. We would especially like to thank Randall Grahm who provided us with excellent feedback. His comments, drawing from his vast knowledge of grape varietes has no doubt made the second edition much better than it otherwise would have been.

Summary of improvements:

1. **Bigger:** The table is now 24 x 36 inches, a whopping 400% larger than the first edition.
2. **Better:** Organized by acidity as well as by weight.
3. **Bigger and Better:** 40 additional grape varieties, for a grand total of 184.
4. **Even Bigger and Better:** The wine indexes have been expanded to include all wine regions and now need their own book.

The only setback to second edition is that it is no longer waterproof. Please use at your own risk.

TABLE OF CONTENTS

WINE CENTURY CLUB

If you've tried at least 100 different grape varieties, you're qualified to join the **Wine Century Club**. Please visit www.delongwine.com/century for details.

INTRODUCTION

This book is the accompanying guide to *De Long's Wine Grape Varietal Table*. Use it to find out which grapes go into which wine as well as an index for locating grape varieties on the chart. The wine indexes, including red, white, rose, sparkling and dessert represent all wine regions worldwide. The grape index lists the 184 grape varieties on the chart as well as popular synonyms.

As the wine world grows, grape varieties become more and more important in all aspects of wine. New regions can't depend on an established history to identify and market their wines; instead the emphasis is on grape variety. Now that the big five classic varieties - Cabernet Sauvignon, Chardonnay, Merlot, Pinot Noir and Sauvignon Blanc - are grown virtually everywhere, winemakers (and wine-marketers) are increasingly using other high quality varieties to distinguish themselves in the marketplace. Syrah/Shiraz and Riesling are also becoming ubiquitous, while local heroes like Sangiovese, Viognier and Barbera are finding new homes around the globe. The net effect is an increased awareness of the almost dizzying number of grape varieties - over 10,000 at last count. Of course, the vast majority doesn't make it past the lab or test garden; the 184 varieties included here represent nearly every grape one can encounter today.

Our intention is to clarify the differences and similarities between grape varieties by putting them together visually, in one eyeshot. The Table is similar in many ways to a periodic table of elements. Grapes really are "elements" that go into making a wine, either alone or blended. Still, the same variety will vary by region, vintage and wine making style so it is important to note that the chart represents an *average, or typical,* weight and acid level for each grape variety. For example, Pinot Noir can be made in a crisp, light Burgundian style or a soft, full bodied Californian style.

Additionally, the table should not be construed as advocating pure varietal wines over blends. Quite the contrary: many of the worlds' greatest wines are blends. Even wines thought of as pure varietals seldom are. By definition, varietals require a minimum percentage of one grape variety. In most of the wine world (including Europe, California and Australia) it's 85%. So a "pure" varietal can have a significant portion of an unmentioned blending partner(s).

We hope you enjoy using the table as much as we enjoyed making it.

Cheers,

Deborah and Steve De Long

HOW TO USE THE WINE GRAPE VARIETAL TABLE

The following information is also printed on the table for your convenience.

ORGANISATION OF THE TABLE
The table is organized top to bottom by weight (or body) and left to right by acidity. Each row of grape varieties represents a distinct weight class, with lighter bodied varieties towards the top and fuller bodied varieties towards the bottom. Varying degrees of acidity are indicated by outlines around each grape variety: a heavy outline indicates high to very high acidity; a medium outline indicates moderate to high acidity

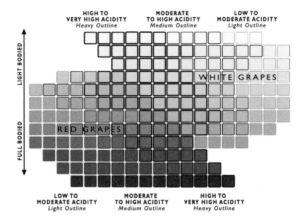

and a light outline indicates low to moderate acidity.
WEIGHT (BODY) OF WINE
The weight of a wine is the sensation of fullness perceived in the mouth through tasting. Combinations of varying concentrations of alcohol, extract, residual sugars and glycerol (only in more full bodied wines) determine whether a wine is more full bodied or light bodied. Tannins levels are usually higher in full bodied wines and add ageability but not body. Also, the weight of a wine is not qualitative: great wines can be either full bodied or light bodied.

ACIDITY OF WINE
Acidity is usually a good thing in a wine, making it refreshing to taste, especially when balanced with enough of the grape's natural sugars. Flabby, or flat, is often describes the opposite of good acid content in a wine. However, just as with body, acidity is not necessarily a mark of quality: there are great wines in all ranges of acid levels.

EFFECTS OF CLIMATE ON BODY AND ACIDITY
The climate has a great impact on the body and acidity of a grape variety. In cool climates, grapes tend to be higher in acidity and lower in body. In hot climates, the opposite is true: grapes grown there tend to be lower in acidity and higher in body. Additionally, timing the harvest has an effect: the earlier the harvest, the less ripe the grape, will result in a higher acidity and lower body while later harvests, with riper grapes will result in lower acidity and greater body.

BALANCE IN WINE

Regardless of acid or weight levels of a grape variety, all winemakers strive for balance. To achieve this they are often permitted - in cold regions - to chaptalise (add sugar) and/or deacidify the fermenting grape juice. In warmer regions, where acidity can be lacking, winemakers are often permitted to add tartaric or sometimes citric acid to the fermenting grape juice. The finest expression of wine has the acids, body (alcohol, extract, residual sugars) and tannins in perfect proportion.

VARIETAL CHARACTER

A wine that's named after the main grape from which it's made is called a varietal. The varietal character refers to the unique set of traits of a grape - such as body, flavour, aroma, color - that can be used to identify the grape variety regardless of where, when or by whom it is grown.

WARNING

The WEIGHT and ACIDITY levels indicated on this table reflect average or typical levels for each grape variety. Actual WEIGHT and ACIDITY levels WILL vary for the same GRAPE VARIETY from wine to wine. This is due to varying climates, vintages and winemaking styles. Please note that the intention is to organize the grape varieties relative to each other as if each were vintified as a dry table wine, without chaptalisation or altering acidity (see BALANCE IN WINE). That said, the table should be used more as a guideline and not to settle arguments.

GRAPE VARIETY INDEX

The Grape Variety Index is for locating grape varieties and their synonyms on the Wine Grape Varietal Table. The table is organized by Weight (in rows) and by Acidity, which is indicated by the beaker symbols:

△ low to moderate acidity

◭ moderate to high acidity

▲ high to very high acidity

Agiorgitiko, row H RED △

Aglianico, row K RED ▲

Airén, row A WHITE ◭

Albana, see Greco (row C WHITE ◭)

Albarin Blanco, see Albariño (row C WHITE ▲)

Albariño, row C WHITE ▲

Aleatico, row I RED △

Alfrocheiro, row H RED ▲

Alfrocheiro Preto, see Alfrocheiro (row H RED ▲)

Alicante Bouschet, row J RED △

Aligoté, row C WHITE ▲

Altesse, see Roussanne (row G WHITE ▲)

Alvarinho, see Albariño (row C WHITE ▲)

Ansonica, see Inzolia (row C WHITE ◭)

Anzonica, see Inzolia (row C WHITE ◭)

Aragón, see Grenache/Garnacha (row L RED △)

Aragónes, see Grenache/Garnacha (row L RED △)

Aragonez, see Tempranillo (row H RED △)

Arinto, row C WHITE ▲

Arneis, row D WHITE △

Assario Branco, see Arinto (row C WHITE ▲)

Assyrtiko, row D WHITE ◭

Auxerrois, row G WHITE △, also a synonym for Malbec (row J RED ◭)

Avesso, row F WHITE ◭

Bacchus, row E WHITE △

Baco Noir, row E RED ▲

Badener, see Portugieser (row F RED △)

Baga, row L RED ▲

Barbera, row H RED ▲

Bartolomeu, see Castelão (row I RED ▲)

Bastardo Espanhol, see Castelão (row I RED ▲)

Bical, row E WHITE ▲

Bidure, see Cabernet Sauvignon (row K RED ◭)

Blauburgunder, see Pinot Noir (row F RED ▲)

Blauer Portugieser, see Portugieser (row F RED △)

Blauer Spätburgunder, see Pinot Noir (row F RED ▲)

Blauer Zweigelt, see Zweigelt (row F RED ◭)

Blaufränkisch, row F RED ▲

Boal, see Bual (row I WHITE △)

Bobal, row L RED ▲

Bombino Bianco, row B WHITE ⚗

Bonarda, row I RED △

Bonarda Piedmontese, see Bonarda (row I RED △)

Borrada das Moscas, see Bical (row E WHITE ⚗)

Bouchet, see Cabernet Franc (row G RED ⚗)

Bourboulenc, row A WHITE ⚗

Brachetto, row D RED ⚗

Braquet, see Brachetto (row D RED ⚗)

Breton, see Cabernet Franc (row G RED ⚗)

Brunello, see Sangiovese (row H RED ▲)

Bual, row I WHITE △

Burgundac Crni, see Pinot Noir (row F RED ▲)

Cabernet Franc, row G RED ⚗

Cabernet Sauvignon, row K RED ⚗

Cadarca, see Kadarka (row G RED ⚗)

Cagnina, see Refosco (row I RED ▲)

Cainho Branco, see Albariño (row C WHITE ▲)

Calabrese, see Nero D'Avola (row L RED ▲)

Canaiolo, row G RED △

Cannonau, see Grenache/Garnacha (row L RED △)

Carignan, row K RED ▲

Carignane, see Carignan (row K RED ▲)

Carignano, see Carignan (row K RED ▲)

Cariñena, see Carignan (row K RED ▲)

Carmenère, row K RED △

Castelão, row I RED ▲

Castelão Francês, see Castelão (row I RED ▲)

Catarratto, row D WHITE ⚗

Catawba, row D RED ▲

Cencibel, see Tempranillo (row H RED △)

Cerceal, see Sercial (row D WHITE ▲)

Charbono, row I RED ⚗

Chardonnay, row H WHITE ▲

Chasselas, row C WHITE △

Chenin Blanc, row G WHITE ▲

Chenin Noir, see Pineau D'Aunis (row F RED ▲)

Chiavennasca, see Nebbiolo (row J RED ▲)

Cinsaut, row K RED ▲

Clairette, row F WHITE △

Coda di Volpe, row F WHITE ⚗

Colombard, row B WHITE ▲

Concord, row H RED ⚗

Cortese, row C WHITE ⚗

Corvina, row F RED ⚗

Cot, see Malbec (row J RED ⚗)

Counoise, row I RED ▲

Cserszegi Fuszeres, row E WHITE △

De Chaunac, row E RED ⚗

Delaware, row B WHITE ⚗

Dolcetto, row I RED △

Dornfelder, row E RED ▲

Douce Noir, see Dolcetto (row I RED △)
Drumin, see Gewürztraminer (row I WHITE △)
Dusty Miller, see Meunier (row I RED ▲)
Erbaluce, row F WHITE ▲
Ermitage, see Marsanne (row H WHITE △)
Esgana Cão, see Sercial (row D WHITE ▲)
Esparte, see Mourvèdre (row L RED ▲)
Falanghina, row E WHITE ▲
Farineux, see Meunier (row I RED ▲)
Fendant, see Chasselas (row C WHITE △)
Feteasca Alba, row B WHITE △
Fer, row H RED ▲
Fer Servadou, see Fer (row H RED ▲)
Fiano, row E WHITE ▲
Folle Blanche, row A WHITE ▲
Francher Kello White, see Catawba (row D RED ▲)
Franconia, see Blaufränkisch (row F RED ▲)
Frankovka, see Blaufränkisch (row F RED ▲)
Fransdruif, see Palomino (row A WHITE △)
Frappato, row E RED ▲
Freisa, row G RED ▲
French Colombard, see Colombard (row B WHITE ▲)
Fumé Blanc, see Sauvignon Blanc (row E WHITE ▲)
Furmint, row H WHITE ▲
Gaglioppo, row I RED △
Gamay, row E RED ▲
Gamza, see Kadarka, (row G RED ▲)
Garganega, row D WHITE △
Garnacha, see Grenache/Garnacha (row L RED △)
Garnacha Blanca, see Grenache Blanc (row F WHITE △)
Garnacha Peluda, see Lladoner Pelut (row L RED △)
Garnacha Tinta, see Grenache/Garnacha (row L RED △)
Garnacha Tintorera, see Alicante Bouschet (row J RED △)
Garnacho Tinto, see Grenache/Garnacha (row L RED △)
Garnaxta, see Grenache/Garnacha (row L RED △)
Gewürztraminer, row I WHITE △
Godello, row D WHITE ▲
Gouveio, see Verdelho (row E WHITE ▲)
Graciano, row J RED △
Granaccia, see Grenache/Garnacha (row L RED △)
Grand Vidure, see Carmenère (row K RED △)
Grasevina, see Welschriesling (row B WHITE ▲**)**
Grauburgunder, see Pinot Gris (row H WHITE ▲)
Grechetto, row G WHITE ▲
Greco, row C WHITE ▲
Grenache Blanc, row F WHITE △
Grenache/Garnacha, row L RED △
Grenache Noir, see Grenache/Garnacha (row L RED △)
Grignolino, row E RED ▲
Grolleau, row D RED ▲
Gros Manseng, row G WHITE ▲

Gros Plant, see Folle Blanche (row A WHITE ▲)
Groslot, see Grolleau (row D RED ▲)
Grosse Roussette, see Marsanne (row H WHITE △)
Grüner Sylvaner, see Silvaner (row B WHITE ▲)
Grüner Veltliner, row F WHITE ▲
Gutedel, see Chasselas (row C WHITE △)
Hanepoot, see Muscat of Alexandria (row E WHITE △)
Hárslevelü, row I WHITE △
Heida, see Gewürztraminer (row I WHITE △)
Heiden, see Gewürztraminer (row I WHITE △)
Hondarrabi Zuri, row A WHITE ▲
Hunter Valley Riesling, see Sémillon (row I WHITE △)
Inzolia, row C WHITE ▲
Irsai Olivér, see Irsay Oliver (row D WHITE △)
Irsay Oliver, row D WHITE △
Johannisberg, see Silvaner (row B WHITE ▲)
Johannisberg Riesling, see Riesling (row A WHITE ▲)
Kadarka, row G RED ▲
Kékfrankos, see Blaufränkisch (row F RED ▲)
Kékoporto, see Portugieser (row F RED △)
Kerner, row A WHITE ▲
Klevner, see Pinot Noir (row F RED ▲)
Lairén, see Airén (row A WHITE ▲)
Lagrein, row K RED ▲
Lambrusco, row D RED ▲
Laski Rizling, see Welschriesling (row B WHITE ▲)
Leányka, see Feteasca Alba (row B WHITE △)
Len de L'El, row G WHITE △
Lemberger, see Blaufränkisch (row F RED ▲)
Lexia, see Muscat of Alexandria (row E WHITE △)
Limberger, see Blaufränkisch (row F RED ▲)
Liwora, see Gewürztraminer (row I WHITE △)
Listán, see Palamino (row A WHITE △)
Lladoner Pelut, row L RED △
Loureira, see Louriero (row A WHITE ▲)
Loureiro, row A WHITE ▲
Macabeo, row D WHITE △
Maccabéo, see Macabeo (row D WHITE △)
Maccabeu, see Macabeo (row D WHITE △)
Mala Dinka, see Gewürztraminer (row I WHITE △)
Malagousia, row H WHITE ▲
Malbec, row J RED ▲
Malbeck, see Malbec (row J RED ▲)
Malmsey, see Malvasia (row F WHITE △)
Malvasia Nera, row H RED ▲
Malvasia, row F WHITE △
Malvazia Fina, see Arinto (row C WHITE ▲)
Malvoisie, synonym for Pinot Gris (row H WHITE ▲), Bourboulenc (row A WHITE ▲), Macabeo (row D WHITE △), Vermentino (row D WHITE ▲)
Mamouth Catawba, see Catawba (row D RED ▲)

GRAPE INDEX

Muskat-Silvaner, see Sauvignon Blanc (row E WHITE ⚱)
Napa Gamay, see Valdiguié (row G RED △)
Nebbiolo, row J RED ▲
Negra Mole, see Tinta Negra Mole (row G RED ▲)
Negramoll, see Tinta Negra Mole (row G RED ▲)
Négrette, row L RED ▲
Negroamaro, row L RED △
Nerello Mascalese, row J RED △
Nero D'Avola, row L RED ▲
Nielluccio, see Sangiovese (row H RED ▲)
Niagara, row D WHITE ⚱
Noirien, see Pinot Noir (row F RED ▲)
Noirin Enfariné, see Meunier (row I RED ▲)
Norton, row J RED ▲
Ojo de Liebre, see Tempranillo (row H RED △)
Olasz Rizling, see Welschriesling (row B WHITE ⚱)
Oporto, see Portugieser (row F RED △)
Ormeasco, see Dolcetto (row I RED △)
Ottavianello, see Cinsaut (row K RED ▲)
Padernã, see Arinto (row C WHITE ▲)
Pagadebit, see Bombino Bianco (row B WHITE ⚱)
Païen, see Gewürztraminer (row I WHITE △)
Palomino, row A WHITE △
Palomino Fino, see Palomino (row A WHITE △)
Pansa Blanca, see Xarel-lo (row E WHITE △)
Parellada, row A WHITE ⚱
Pé de Rato, see Alfrocheiro (row H RED ▲)
Pedro Ximénez, row A WHITE △
Pere'e Pallummo, see Piedirosso (row I RED ⚱)
Periquita, see Castelão (row I RED ▲)
Perlan, see Chasselas (row C WHITE △)
Petit Manseng, row H WHITE ⚱
Petit Verdot, row K RED ▲
Petite Arvine, row G WHITE ▲
Petite Sirah, row K RED ⚱
Petite Vidure, see Cabernet Sauvignon (row K RED ⚱)
Picapoll, see Picpoul Blanc (row F WHITE ▲)
Picpoul Blanc, row F WHITE ▲
Picutener, see Nebbiolo (row J RED ▲)
Piedirosso, row I RED ⚱
Pigato, row B WHITE ▲
Pignolo, row L RED ⚱
Pinat Cervena, see Gewürztraminer (row I WHITE △)
Pineau, see Chenin Blanc (row G WHITE ▲)
Pineau D'Aunis, row F RED ▲
Pineau de la Loire, see Chenin Blanc (row G WHITE ▲)
Pinot Beurot, see Pinto Gris (row H WHITE ⚱)
Pinot Bianco, see Pinot Blanc (row F WHITE ▲)
Pinot Blanc, row F WHITE ▲
Pinot Chardonnay, see Chardonnay (row H WHITE ▲)
Pinot Grigio, see Pinto Gris (row H WHITE ⚱)

Pinot Gris, row H WHITE △

Pinot Meunier, see Meunier (row I RED ▲)

Pinot Nero, see Pinot Noir (row F RED ▲)

Pinot Noir, row F RED ▲

Pinot St George, see Négrette (row L RED △)

Pinotage, row K RED △

Piquepoul, see Folle Blanche (row A WHITE ▲)

Plavac Mali, row J RED △

Portugais Bleu, see Portugieser (row F RED △)

Portugaljka, see Portugieser (row F RED △)

Portugieser, row F RED △

Pressac, see Malbec (row J RED △)

Preto Martinho, see Tinta Negra Mole (row G RED ▲)

Primitivo, see Zinfandel/Primitivo (row L RED △)

Princ, see Gewürztraminer (row I WHITE △)

Prosecco, row A WHITE △

Prugnolo Gentile, see Sangiovese (row H RED ▲)

Refosco, row I RED ▲

Rhein Riesling, see Riesling (row A WHITE ▲)

Rhine Riesling, see Riesling (row A WHITE ▲)

Rhoditis, see Roditis (row B WHITE △)

Ribolla Nera, see Schioppettino (row J RED ▲)

Riesling, row A WHITE ▲

Riesling Italico, see Welschriesling (row B WHITE △)

Riesling Retano, see Riesling (row A WHITE ▲)

Rivaner, see Müller-Thurgau (row A WHITE △)

Rizling Vlassky, see Welschriesling (row B WHITE △)

Rkatsiteli, row C WHITE ▲

Roditis, row B WHITE △

Rondinella, row F RED △

Rossola Bianca, see Trebbiano/Ugni Blanc (row B WHITE ▲)

Rotclevner, see Gewürztraminer (row I WHITE △)

Roter Traminer, see Gewürztraminer (row I WHITE △)

Rouchet, see Ruché (row G RED △)

Roussanne, row G WHITE ▲

Roussette, see Roussanne (row G WHITE ▲)

Ruby Cabernet, row K RED △

Ruché, row G RED △

Ruländer, see Pinot Gris (row H WHITE △)

Rusa, see Gewürztraminer (row I WHITE △)

St-Émilion, see Trebbiano/Ugni Blanc (row B WHITE ▲)

St. Laurent, row F RED △

Sagrantino, row J RED ▲

Sämling 88, see Scheurebe (row B WHITE ▲)

Sangiovese, row H RED ▲

Sangioveto, see Sangiovese (row H RED ▲)

Saperavi, row H RED ▲

Sauvignon Blanc, row E WHITE ▲

Savagnin, row C WHITE ▲

Savagnin Noir, see Pinot Noir (row F RED ▲)

Savatiano, row B WHITE △

Scheurebe, row B WHITE ▲

Schiava, row D RED △

Schioppettino, row J RED ▲

Schönburger, row G WHITE △

Schwartzriesling, see Meunier (row I RED ▲)

Sémillon, row I WHITE △

Sercial, row D WHITE ▲

Seyval Blanc, row D WHITE ▲

Shiraz, see Syrah/Shiraz (row L RED ▲)

Silvaner, row B WHITE ▲

Spanna, see Nebbiolo (row J RED ▲)

Spätburgunder, see Pinot Noir (row F RED ▲)

Steen, see Chenin Blanc (row G WHITE ▲)

Straccia Cambiale, see Bombino Bianco (row B WHITE ▲)

Sylvaner, see Silvaner (row B WHITE ▲)

Syrah/Shiraz, row L RED ▲

Szürkebarát, see Pinto Gris (row H WHITE ▲)

Tannat, row J RED ▲

Tempranilla, see Tempranillo (row H RED △)

Tempranillo, row H RED △

Termano Aromatico, see Gewürztraminer (row I WHITE △)

Teroldego, row I RED ▲

Teroldego Rotaliano, see Teroldego (row I RED ▲)

Thalia, see Trebbiano/Ugni Blanc (row B WHITE ▲)

Tinta Amarela, row H RED △

Tinta Aragonez, see Tempranillo (row H RED △)

Tinta Bairrada, see Baga (row L RED ▲)

Tinta Barroca, row J RED △

Tinta de Baga, see Baga (row L RED ▲)

Tinta Fina, see Baga (row L RED ▲)

Tinta Madeira, see Tinta Negra Mole (row G RED ▲)

Tinta Merousa, see Castelão (row I RED ▲)

Tinta Negra Mole, row G RED ▲

Tinta Roriz, see Tempranillo (row H RED △)

Tinto Aragonés, see Grenache/Garnacha (row L RED △)

Tinto Cão, row G RED △

Tinto de Madrid, see Tempranillo (row H RED △)

Tinto del País, see Tempranillo (row H RED △)

Tinto de la Rioja, see Tempranillo (row H RED △)

Tinto de Santiago, see Tempranillo (row H RED △)

Tinto de Toro, see Tempranillo (row H RED △)

Tocai Fruilano, row C WHITE ▲

Tokay, see Muscadelle (row C WHITE △)

Tokay d'Alsace, see Pinto Gris (row H WHITE ▲)

Tokay-Pinot Gris, see Pinto Gris (row H WHITE ▲)

Torrontés, row E WHITE ▲

Touriga Franca, row J RED ▲

Touriga Francesa, see Touriga Franca (row J RED ▲)

Touriga Nacional, row L RED ▲

Traminac, see Gewürztraminer (row I WHITE △)

Traminer Aromatico, see Gewürztraminer (row I WHITE △)

WINE INDEXES (what grape are you drinking?)

On most bottles of European wines you won't find the name of the grape variety (or varieties). Instead, they're named for the place they come from - the appelllation - be it a region or village. Use the wine indexes to find out which grape goes into which wine: they're organized in red, white, rosé, sparkling and dessert wines.

The **Appellations** are listed alphabetically in bold along with their REGION and COUNTRY, followed by the grape varieties officially permitted in the wines (parentheses indicate grape varieties permitted but seldom used or only in small amounts). Grape varietes not on the Wine Grape Varietal Table are indicated by *italics*. Percentages are indicated where applicable.

RED WINES INDEX

Abona SPAIN *Listán Negro, Negramoll,* (*Bastardo Negro,* Malvasía Negra, Moscatel Negro, *Tintilla, Vijariego Negro*)

Acqui PIEDMONT, ITA Brachetto

Agioritikos GREECE Cabernet Sauvignon, *Limnio,* Sauvignon Blanc

Aglianico del Taburno CAMPANIA, ITA Aglianico 85%, (other local red varieties 15% max)

Aglianico del Vulture BASILICATA, ITA Aglianico

Ajaccio CORSICA, FRA *Sciacarello, Barbarossa, Nielluccio,* Vermentino, (Grenache, Cinsaut, Carignan)

Albugnano PIEDMONT, ITA Nebbiolo 85% (Freisa, Barbera and/or Bonarda 15% max)

Alcamo SICILY, ITA Nero d'Avola 60% min, Sangiovese, Frappato, *Perricone,* Cabernet Sauvignon, Merlot and/or Syrah 40% max (other local varieties 10% max)

Alcobaço PORTUGAL Castelão, Baga, Trincadeira 60% min with Castelão at 50% min, other local varieties 40% max

Alella SPAIN Tempranillo, Garnacha, (Garnacha Peluda, Cabernet Sauvignon, Merlot, Pinot Noir)

Alenquer PORTUGAL Aragonez, Castelão, *Tinta Miúda,* Touriga Nacional and/or Trincadeira 65% min, *Camarate, Jaén, Preto Martinho,* Syrah, Tinta Barroca and/or Touriga Franca 35% max, (Alicante Bouschet, *Amostrinha,* Baga, Cabernet Sauvignon, *Caladoc* 15% max)

Alentejo Borba PORTUGAL Aragonez, Castelão and/or Trincadeira 75% min, Alfrocheiro, Alicante Bouschet, Cabernet Sauvignon, Carignan, *Grand Noir, Moreto* and/or *Tinta Caiada* 25% max

Alentejo Évora PORTUGAL Aragonez, Castelão, *Tinta Caiada,* and/or Trincadeira 75% min, Alfrocheiro, Alicante Bouschet, Cabernet Sauvignon, Carignan, *Grand Noir* and/or *Moreto* 25% max

Alentejo Granja/Amareleja PORTUGAL Alfrocheiro, Aragonez, Castelão and/or *Moreto* 80% min, (Carignan, *Tinta Caiada* and/or Trincadeira 20% max)

Alentejo Moura PORTUGAL Alfrocheiro, Aragonez, Castelão, *Moreto* and/or Trincadeira 75% min, Alicante Bouschet, Cabernet Sauvignon and/or *Tinta Carvalha* 25% max

Alentejo Portalegre PORTUGAL Aragonez, Castelão, *Grand Noir* and/or Trincadeira 75% min, Alicante Bouschet, Cinsaut and/or *Moreto* 25% max

Alentejo Redondo PORTUGAL Alfrocheiro, Aragonez, Castelão, *Tinta Caiada* and/or Trincadeira 70% min, Alicante Bouschet, Cabernet Sauvignon, Carignan, *Grand Noir* and/or *Moreto* 30% max

Alentejo Reguengos PORTUGAL Aragonez, Castelão, *Tinta Caiada* and/or Trincadeira 70% min, Alfrocheiro, Alicante Bouschet, Cabernet Sauvignon, Carignan, *Corropio*, *Grand Noir* and/or *Moreto* 30% max

Alentejo Vidigueira PORTUGAL Alfrocheiro, Aragonez, Castelão, *Grossa, Moreto* and/or Trincadeira 75% min, Alicante Bouschet, Cabernet Sauvignon and/or *Tinta Caiada* 25% max

Alghero SARDINIA, ITA One or more local non-aromatic red varieties 100%

Alezio APULIA, ITA Negroamaro 80% min, (Malvasia Nera, Montepulciano, *Sangiovese*)

Alicante SPAIN Monastrell, Bobal, Garnacha (Garnacha Tintorera, Tempranillo, Cabernet Sauvignon, Merlot, Syrah, Pinot Noir)

Almansa SPAIN Monastrell, Garnacha Tintorera, Tempranillo, (Cabernet Sauvignon)

Aloxe Corton BURGUNDY, FRA Pinot Noir, (Pinot Gris and Pinot Liébault allowed but virtually never used)

Alto Adige Colli di Bolzano ALTO ADIGE, ITA Schiava 90% min, (Lagrein, Pinot Nero)

Alto Adige Lago di Caldaro ALTO ADIGE, ITA Schiava 85% min, (Lagrein, Pinot Nero)

Alto Adige Meranese ALTO ADIGE, ITA Schiava 85% min, (Lagrein, Pinot Nero)

Alto Adige Santa Maddalena ALTO ADIGE, ITA Schiava 85% min, (Lagrein, Pinot Nero)

Ampurdán-Costa Brava SPAIN Cariñena, Garnacha, Tempranillo, Cabernet Sauvignon, Merlot, (Syrah)

Amynteon / Amyndaio GREECE Xynomavro

Anjou LOIRE, FRA Cabernet Franc, (Cabernet Sauvignon, Pineau d'Aunis)

Anjou-Villages LOIRE, FRA Cabernet Franc, (Cabernet Sauvignon)

Amarone VENETO, ITA Corvina 40%-70%, Rondinella 20-40%, Molinara 5-25%, (Barbera, *Negrara Trentina, Rossignola,* Sangiovese)

Arbois JURA, FRA *Poulsard, Trousseau,* Pinot Noir

Arborea SARDINIA, ITA Sangiovese

Arbois Pupillin JURA, FRA *Poulsard, Trousseau,* Pinot Noir

Archanes GREECE *Kotsifali, Mandelaria*

Arcole VENETO, ITA Merlot 50% min, other local non-aromatic red varieties 50% max

Archanes / Arhánes GREECE Kotsifáli, Mandylariá

Arruda PORTUGAL Aragonez, Castelão, *Tinta Miúda*, Touriga Nacional and/or Trincadeira 70% min, Alicante Bouschet, Cabernet Sauvignon, *Camarate, Jaén,* Syrah, Tinta Barroca and/or Touriga Franca 30% max, (*Caladoc* 15% max)

Assisi UMBRIA, ITA Sangiovese 50-70%, other local red varieties 40% max, (Merlot 10-30%)

Atina LATIUM, ITA Cabernet Sauvignon 50%, Syrah 10%, Merlot 10%, Cabernet Franc 10%, (other local red varieties 20% max)

Auxey-Duresses BURGUNDY, FRA Pinot Noir, (Pinot Gris and Pinot Liébault allowed but virtually never used)

Bagnoli (di Sopra) VENETO, ITA Merlot 15-60%, Cabernet Franc, Cabernet Sauvignon and/or Carmenere 15% min, *Raboso Piave* and/or *Raboso Veronese* 15% min, (other local non-aromatic red varieties 10% max)

Bairrada PORTUGAL Baga, Alfrocheiro, *Camarate*, Castelão, *Jaén* and/or Touriga Nacional 85% min w/ Baga at 50% min, (Aragonez, *Bastardo*, Cabernet Sauvignon, Merlot, Pinot Noir, *Rufete*, Syrah, Tinta Barroca, Tinto Cão, Touriga Franca)

Bairrada Clássico PORTUGAL Baga 50% min, Alfrocheiro, *Camarate*, Castelão, *Jaén*, Touriga Nacional

Bandol PROVENCE, FRA Mourvèdre 50% min, Grenache, Cinsaut, (Syrah, Carignan)

Barbaresco PIEDMONT, ITA Nebbiolo

Bardolino VENETO, ITA Corvina 35-65%, Rondinella 10-40%, (Molinara 10-20%, *Negrara* 10%, *Rossignola*, Barbera, Sangiovese, Garganega 15% max)

Bardolino Superiore VENETO, ITA Corvina 35-65%, Rondinella 10-40%, (Molinara, *Rossignola*, Barbera, Sangiovese, Marzemino, Cabernet Sauvignon)

Barbera d'Alba PIEDMONT, ITA Barbera

Barbera d'Asti PIEDMONT, ITA Barbera 85-100%, (Freisa, Grignolino and/or Dolcetto 15% max)

Barbera del Monferrato PIEDMONT, ITA Barbera 85% (Freisa and/or Grignolino and/or Dolcetto 15% max

Barco Reale di Carmignano TUSCANY, ITA Sangiovese 50%, Canaiolo 20%, (Cabernet franc and/or Cabernet sauvignon, 10-20%, Trebbiano, *Canaiolo Bianco*, and/or Malvasia del Chianti 10% max, other local red varieties 10% max)

Barolo PIEDMONT, ITA Nebbiolo

Béarn SOUTHWEST, FRA Tannat, (Cabernet Sauvignon, Cabernet Franc, Fer, *Manseng Noir, Courbu Noir*)

Beira Interior Castelo Rodrigo PORTUGAL Aragonez, *Bastardo, Marufo, Rufete* and/or Touriga Nacional 80% min, (Baga, Tinta Carvalha, Pilongo and/or Trincadeira 20% max)

Beira Interior Cova da Beira PORTUGAL Aragonez, Baga, *Bastardo, Jaén, Marufo, Moreto,* Castelão, *Rufete, Tinta Carvalha,* Touriga Nacional and/or Trincadeira 80% min, (Alfrocheiro 20% max)

Bergerac SOUTHWEST, FRA Cabernet Sauvignon, Cabernet Franc, Merlot, (Malbec, Fer, *Mérille*)

Beaujolais BURGUNDY, FRA Gamay (Pinot Noir, Pinot Gris)

Beaujolais Supérieur BURGUNDY, FRA Gamay (Pinot Noir, Pinot Gris)

Beaujolais-Villages BURGUNDY, FRA Gamay (Pinot Noir, Pinot Gris)

Beaune BURGUNDY, FRA Pinot Noir, (Pinot Gris and Pinot Liébault allowed but virtually never used)

Bellet PROVENCE, FRA Braquet, *Fuella,* Cinsaut, (Grenache, *Rolle,* Ugni Blanc, *Mayorquin,* Clairette, Bourboulenc, Chardonnay, *Pignerol,* Muscat Blanc)

Bierzo SPAIN *Doña Mencía* 70% min (Garnacha Tintorera, Cabernet Sauvignon, Merlot, Pinot Noir, Tempranillo)

Biferno MOLISES, ITA Montepulciano 60-70%, Trebbiano Toscano 15-20%, Aglianico 15-20%, (other local varieties 5% max)

Binissalem SPAIN *Manto Negro* 50% min, Callet, Tempranillo, Monastrell

Bivongi CALABRIA, ITA Gaglioppo and/or *Greco Nero* 30-50%, *Nocera* and/or Calabrese 30-50%, (other local red varieties 10% max, other local white varieties 15% max)

Bizkaiako Txacoli SPAIN *Hondarrabi Beltza*

Blagny BURGUNDY, FRA Pinot Noir, (Pinot Gris and Pinot Liébault allowed but virtually never used)

Blaye BORDEAUX, FRA Cabernet Sauvignon, Cabernet Franc, Merlot, Malbec, (*Prolongeau, Béquignol,* Petit Verdot)

Boca PIEDMONT, ITA Nebbiolo 45-70%, *Vespolina* 20-40% (*Bonarda Novarese* 20% max)

Bolgheri TUSCANY, ITA Cabernet Sauvignon 10-80%, Merlot 80% max, Sangiovese 70% max, other local red varieties 30% max

Bolgheri Sassicaia TUSCANY, ITA Cabernet Sauvignon 80%, (other local red varieties 20% max)

Bonnes-Mares BURGUNDY, FRA Pinot Noir, (Pinot Gris and Pinot Liébault allowed but virtually never used)

Bordeaux BORDEAUX, FRA Cabernet Sauvignon, Cabernet Franc, Merlot, (Malbec, Petit Verdot, Carmenère)

> **Mouton Cadet Rouge**, the most famous Bordeaux Rouge, is a typical Bordeaux blend of 55% Merlot, 30% Cabernet Sauvignon and 15% Cabernet Franc.

Bordeaux Côtes de Francs BORDEAUX, FRA Cabernet Sauvignon, Cabernet Franc, Merlot, (Malbec)

Bordeaux Supérieur BORDEAUX, FRA Cabernet Sauvignon, Cabernet Franc, Merlot, (Malbec, Petit Verdot, Carmenère)

Botticino LOMBARDY, ITA Barbera 30% (Marzemino 20%, Schiava Gentile 10%, Sangiovese 10%, other local red varieties 10% max)

Bourg BORDEAUX, FRA Cabernet Sauvignon, Cabernet Franc, Merlot, Malbec, (*Prolongeau, Gros Verdot*)

Bourgogne BURGUNDY, FRA Pinot Noir, (Pinot Gris, Pinot Liébault, *César, Tressot*)

Bourgogne Hautes-Côtes de Nuits BURGUNDY, FRA Pinot Noir, (Pinot Liébault, Pinot Gris)

Bourgogne Grand Ordinaire BURGUNDY, FRA Pinot Noir, Gamay, (*César, Tressot*)

Bourgogne Hautes-Côtes de Nuits BURGUNDY, FRA Pinot Noir, (Pinot Liébault, Pinot Gris)

Bourgogne Passetoutgrains BURGUNDY, FRA Pinot Noir, Gamay 33% max, (Chardonnay, Pinot Blanc, Pinot Gris 15% max)

Bourgeais BORDEAUX, FRA Cabernet Sauvignon, Cabernet Franc, Merlot, Malbec, (*Prolongeau, Gros Verdot*)

Bourgueil LOIRE, FRA Cabernet Franc 90-100%, (Cabernet Sauvignon)

Brachetto d'Acqui PIEDMONT, ITA Brachetto

Bramaterra PIEDMONT, ITA Nebbiolo 50-70%, *Croatina* 20-30%, (Bonarda and/or *Vespolina* 20% max)

Breganze VENETO, ITA Merlot 85%, (other local non-aromatic red varieties 15% max)

Brézème-Côtes-du-Rhône RHÔNE, FRA Syrah

Brindisi APULIA, ITA Negroamaro 70% min (Montepulciano, Malvasia Nera, Sangiovese, *Susumaniello)*

Brouilly BURGUNDY, FRA Gamay, (Chardonnay, Aligoté, Melon de Bourgogne)

Brunello di Montalcino TUSCANY, ITA Sangiovese

Bullas SPAIN Monastrell, (Tempranillo, Garnacha, Cabernet Sauvignon, Merlot, Syrah)

Bull's Blood of Eger HUNGARY Kékfrankos, Cabernet Sauvignon, Merlot, Kékoportó, (Kadarka)

Buzet SOUTHWEST, FRA Merlot, Cabernet Sauvignon, Cabernet Franc, Malbec

Cabardès LANGUEDOC-ROUSSILLON, FRA Cinsaut, Grenache, Syrah, (Merlot, Cabernet Sauvignon, Cabernet Franc, Malbec, Fer)

Cacc'e Mmitte di Lucera APULIA, ITA Uva di Troia 35%-60%, Montepulciano, Sangiovese, and/or Malvasia Nera 25%-35%, Trebbiano, Bombino Bianco, and/or Malvasia 15%-30%

Cahors SOUTHWEST, FRA Malbec 70% min, (Merlot, Tannat)

Calatayud SPAIN Garnacha, Mazuelo, Tempranillo, (Monastrel, Cabernet Sauvignon, Syrah)

Caldaro TRENTINO-ALTO ADIGE, ITA Schiava 85-100% (Pinot Noir and/or Lagrein 15% max)

Campi Flegrei CAMPANIA, ITA Piedirosso 50-70%, Aglianico and/or *Sciascinoso* 10-30%, (other local red varieties 10% max)

Campidano di Terralba SARDINIA, ITA *Bovale di Spagna* and/or *Bovale Sardo* 80% min, (*Pascale di Cagliari, Greco* and/or Monica 20% max)

Campo de Borja SPAIN Garnacha 50% min, Tempranillo, (Mazuelo, Cabernet Sauvugnon, Merlot, Syrah)

Canasium APULIA, ITA Uva di Troia 65% min, Sangiovese and/or Montepulciano 35% max, (other local red varieties 5% max)

Cannonau di Sardegna SARDINIA, ITA Grenache 90%, (other local red varieties 10% max)

Canavese PIEDMONT, ITA Nebbiolo, Barbera, Bonarda, Freisa and/or *Neretto* 60% min, other local red varieties 40% max

Canon Fronsac BORDEAUX, FRA Cabernet Sauvignon, Cabernet Franc, Merlot, (Malbec)

Capalbio TUSCANY, ITA Sangiovese 50% min, other local non-aromatic red varieties 50% max

Capri CAMPANIA, ITA Piedirosso 80% min, (other local red varieties 20% max)

Capriano del Colle LOMBARDY, ITA Sangiovese 40% min, Marzemino 35% min, (Barbera 3% min, Merlot and/or *Incrocio Terzi* 15% max)

Carema PIEDMONT, ITA Nebbiolo 85% (other local non-aromatic red varieties 15% max)

Carignano del Sulcis SARDINIA, ITA Carignan 85% min, (other local red varieties 15% max)

Cariñena SPAIN Garnacha, Tempranillo, (Cariñena, *Juan Ibáñez*, Monsatrell, Cabernet Sauvignon)

> **Cariñena**, the grape variety known in France as Carignan and one of the most planted varieties worldwide, accounts for only 6% of the vineyard in its namesake appellation.

Carso FRIULI-VENEZIA GIULIA, ITA Refosco 70% min, other local red varieties 30% max

Cassis PROVENCE, FRA Grenache, Carignan, Mourvèdre, Cinsaut, *Barbaroux (Terret, Aramon)*

Castel del Monte APULIA, ITA Uva di Troia 65% min, (Sangiovese, Montepulciano, Aglianico, Pinot Nero)

Castel San Lorenzo CAMPANIA, ITA Barbera 60-80%, Sangiovese 20-30%, (other local red varieties 20% max)

Casteller TRENTINO-ALTO ADIGE, ITA Schiava 30-100%, Lambrusco 60% max, (Merlot, Lagrein and/or Teroldego 20% max)

Castelli Romani LATIUM, ITA *Cesanese*, Merlot, Montepulciano, *Nero Buono* and/or Sangiovese 85% min, (other local red varieties 15% max)

Cellatica LOMBARDY, ITA Barbera 30% min, Marzemino 30% min, (Schiava 10% min, *Incrocio Terzi* 10% min)

Cerasuolo di Vittoria SICILY, ITA Frappato 40% min, Nero d'Avola 60% min, (*Grosso Nero* and/or Nerello Mascalese 10% max)

Cerveteri LATIUM, ITA Sangiovese and/or Montepulciano 60%, *Cesanese* 25%, Canaiolo, Carignano and Barbera 30% max

Cesanese del Piglio LATIUM, ITA *Cesanese di Affile* and/or *Cesanese Comune* 90% min, (Sangiovese, Montepulciano, Barbera, Trebbiano Toscano and/or Bombino Bianco 10% max)

Cesanese di Affile LATIUM, ITA *Cesanese di Affile* and/or *Cesanese Comune* 90% min, (Sangiovese, Montepulciano, Barbera, Trebbiano Toscano and/or Bombino Bianco 10% max)

Cesanese di Olevano Romano LATIUM, ITA *Cesanese di Affile* and/or *Cesanese Comune* 90% min, (Sangiovese, Montepulciano, Barbera, Trebbiano Toscano and/or Bombino Bianco 10% max)

Chacolí de Guetaria SPAIN *Hondarrabi Beltza*

Chacolí de Vizcaya SPAIN *Hondarrabi Beltza*

Chambertin BURGUNDY, FRA Pinot Noir, (Pinot Gris and Pinot Liébault allowed but virtually never used)

Chambertin-Clos-de-Bèze BURGUNDY, FRA Pinot Noir, (Pinot Gris and Pinot Liébault allowed but virtually never used)

Chambolle-Musigny BURGUNDY, FRA Pinot Noir, (Pinot Gris and Pinot Liébault allowed but virtually never used)

Chapelle-Chambertin BURGUNDY, FRA Pinot Noir, (Pinot Gris and Pinot Liébault allowed but virtually never used)

Charmes-Chambertin BURGUNDY, FRA Pinot Noir, (Pinot Gris and Pinot Liébault allowed but virtually never used)

Chassagne-Montrachet BURGUNDY, FRA Pinot Noir, (Pinot Gris and Pinot Liébault allowed but virtually never used)

Châteaumeillant LOIRE, FRA Gamay, (Pinot Gris, Pinot Noir)

Châteauneuf-du-Pape RHÔNE, FRA Grenache, Syrah, Mourvèdre, Cinsaut, *Terret Noir*, (Counoise, *Picpoul Noir*, *Muscardin*, *Picardin*, *Vaccarèse*, Clairette, Roussanne, Bourboulenc)

> **Vieux Télégraphe**, a famous Châteauneuf-du-Pape, is typically 65% Grenache, 15% Mourvèdre, 15% Syrah, and 5% Cinsaut/other varieties.

Châtillon-en-Diois RHÔNE, FRA Gamay (Syrah, Pinot Noir)

Chaves PORTUGAL *Bastardo, Tinta Carvalha* and/or Trincadeira 70% min, other local varieties 30% max

Chénas BURGUNDY, FRA Gamay

Cheverny LOIRE, FRA Gamay 40-65%, (Pinot Noir, Cabernet Franc, Malbec)

Chianti TUSCANY, ITA Sangiovese 75-100%, (Canaiolo Nero max 10%, Trebbiano Toscano and/or Malvasia del Chianti max 10%, other local red varieties 10% max)

Chianti Classico TUSCANY, ITA Sangiovese 80-100%, (other local red varieties 20% max)

Chinon LOIRE, FRA Cabernet Franc 75-100%, (Cabernet Sauvignon)

Chiroubles BURGUNDY, FRA Gamay

Chorey-lés-Beaune BURGUNDY, FRA Pinot Noir, (Pinot Gris and Pinot Liébault allowed but virtually never used)

Cigales SPAIN Tempranillo and/or Garnacha 85% min (Verdejo, Viura, Palomino and/or *Albillo* 15% max)

Cilento CAMPANIA, ITA Aglianico 60-75%, (Piedirosso and/or Primitivo 15-20%, Barbera 10-20%, other local red varieties 10% max)

Cisterna d'Asti Piedmont, ITA *Croatina* 80-100%, (other local non-aromatic red varieties 20% max)

Circeo LATIUM, ITA Merlot 85% min, (other local red varieties 15% max)

Cirò CALABRIA, ITA Gaglioppo 95% min, (Trebbiano, Greco Bianco, Cabernet Sauvignon)

Clos de la Roche BURGUNDY, FRA Pinot Noir, (Pinot Gris and Pinot Liébault allowed but virtually never used)

Clos de Tart BURGUNDY, FRA Pinot Noir, (Pinot Gris and Pinot Liébault allowed but virtually never used)

Clos de Vougeot BURGUNDY, FRA Pinot Noir, (Pinot Gris and Pinot Liébault allowed but virtually never used)

Clos des Lambrays BURGUNDY, FRA Pinot Noir, (Pinot Gris and Pinot Liébault allowed but virtually never used)

Clos St-Denis BURGUNDY, FRA Pinot Noir, (Pinot Gris and Pinot Liébault allowed but virtually never used)

Colares PORTUGAL Ramisco - grown in sand - 80% min (other local varieties 20% max)

Colli Altotiberini UMBRIA, IT Sangiovese 55-70%, (Merlot 10-20%, Trebbiano Toscano and/or Malvasia del Chianti 10%, other local red varieties 15% max)

Colli Amerini UMBRIA, ITA Sangiovese 65-80%, Montepulciano, *Ciliegiolo*, Canaiolo, Merlot and/or Barbera 30% max, (other local red varieties 15% max)

Colli Berici VENETO, ITA The following varietal wines are also made: Cabernet, Merlot, *Tocai Rosso*

Colli Bolognesi EMILIA-ROMAGNA, ITA The following varietal wines are also made: Cabernet Sauvignon, Merlot, Barbera

Colli del Trasimeno UMBRIA, ITA Sangiovese 40%, *Ciliegiolo*, Gamay, Merlot and/or Cabernet Sauvignon 30%, other local red varieties 30% max

Colli della Romagna Centrale EMILIA-ROMAGNA, ITA Cabernet Sauvignon 50-60%, Sangiovese, Barbera, Merlot and/or Montepulciano 40-50%

Colli della Sabina LATIUM, ITA Sangiovese 40-70%, Montepulciano 15-40%, other local red varieties 30% max

Colli dell'Etruria Centrale TUSCANY, ITA Sangiovese 50%, Cabernet Franc, Cabernet Sauvignon, Merlot, Pinot Nero or Canaiolo Nero 50% max, other local varieties 25% max

Colli d'Imola EMILIA-ROMAGNA, ITA Barbera, Cabernet Sauvignon, Sangiovese

Colli di Conegliano VENETO, ITA Cabernet Franc, Cabernet Sauvignon and/or Marzemino 10% min each, Merlot 10-40%, (*Incrocio Manzoni* 10% max)

Colli di Faenza EMILIA-ROMAGNA, ITA Cabernet Sauvignon 40-60%, *Ancellotta*, *Ciliegiolo*, Merlot and/or Sangiovese 40-60%

Colli di Luni LIGURIA & TUSCANY, ITA Sangiovese 60-70%, other local red varieties 25% max (Canaiolo, *Pollera Nera* and/or *Ciliegiolo Nero* 15% min)

Colli di Parma EMILIA-ROMAGNA, ITA Barbera 60-75%, Bonarda and/or *Croatina* 25-40%, (other red grape varieties 15% max). The following varietal wines are also made: Barbera, Bonarda, Cabernet Franc, Cabernet Sauvignon, Lambrusco, Merlot, Pinot Nero

Colli di Rimini EMILIA-ROMAGNA, ITA Sangiovese 60-75%, Cabernet Sauvignon 15-25%, Merlot, Barbera, Montepulciano, *Ciliegiolo*, *Terrano* and/or *Ancellotta* 25% min

Colli di Scandiano e Canossa EMILIA-ROMAGNA, ITA The following varietal wines are also made: Cabernet Sauvignon, Lambrusco, *Malbo Gentile*

Colli Etruschi Viterbesi LATIUM, ITA Sangiovese 50-65%, Montepulciano 20-45%, other local red varieties 30% max. The following varietal wines are also made: Canaiolo, Merlot, Sangiovese, *Greghetto*, *Violone*

Colli Euganei VENETO, ITA Merlot 60-80%, Cabernet Franc, Cabernet Sauvignon, Barbera and/or *Raboso Veronese* 20-40%

Colli Maceratesi MARCHES, ITA Sangiovese 50%, Cabernet Franc, Cabernet Sauvignon, *Ciliegiolo*, *Lacrima*, Merlot, Montepulciano and/or *Vernaccia Nera* 50% max (other local red varieties 15% max)

Colli Martani UMBRIA, ITA Sangiovese 85%, (Canaiolo, Barbera, Merlot, Montepulciano, Ciliegiolo, Trebbiano, Grechetto, Malvasia, Garganega and/or Verdicchio 15% max, of which white grapes 10% max)

Colli Orientali del Friuli FRIULI-VENEZIA GIULIA, ITA One or more local red varieties as a blend. The following varietal wines are also made: Cabernet Sauvignon, Cabernet Franc, Merlot, Pignolo, Pinot Nero, Refosco, Schioppettino, *Tazzelenghe*

Colli Perugini Umbria, ITA Sangiovese 50% min, other local red varieties 50% max. The following varietal wines are also made: Cabernet Sauvignon, Merlot, Sangiovese

Colli Pesaresi Marches, ITA Sangiovese 70% min, other local non-aromatic red varieties 30% max

Colli Pesaresi Focara Pinot Nero Marches, ITA Pinot Nero min 90%, (other local non-aromatic red varieties 10% max)

Colli Pesaresi Focara Rosso Marches, ITA Pinot Nero, Cabernet Sauvignon, Cabernet Franc and/or Merlot 50%, Sangiovese 50% max, other local non-aromatic red varieties 25% max

Colli Piacentini EMILIA-ROMAGNA, ITA The following varietal wines are also made: Barbera, Bonarda, Cabernet Sauvignon, Pinot Nero

Colli Piacentini Gutturnio EMILIA-ROMAGNA, ITA Barbera 55-70%, *Croatina* 30-45%

Colli Piacentini Novello EMILIA-ROMAGNA, ITA Pinot Nero, Barbera and/or *Croatina* 60%; other local red varieties 40% max

Colli Tortonesi PIEDMONT, ITA One or more local non-aromatic red varieties as a blend. The following varietal wines are also made: Barbera, Dolcetto

Collina Torinese PIEDMONT, ITA Barbera 60% min, Freisa 25% min (other local non-aromatic red varieties 5% max). The following varietal wines are also made: Barbera, Bonarda, *Pelaverga*

Colline di Levanto LIGURIA, ITA Sangiovese 40%, other local red varieties 40% max, (*Ciliegiolo* 20%)

Colline Lucchesi TUSCANY, ITA Sangiovese 45-70%, Canaiolo and/or Ciliegiolo 30%, (Merlot 15% max, other local red varieties 15% max). The following varietal wines are also made: Sangiovese, Merlot

Colline Novaresi PIEDMONT, ITA Nebbiolo 30%, *Uva Rara* 40% max, *Vespolina* and/or *Croatina* 30% max. The following varietal wines are also made: Nebbiolo, Barbera, *Croatina, Uva Rara, Vespolina*

Colline Saluzzesi PIEDMONT, ITA *Pelaverga*, Nebbiolo and/or Barbera 60%, other local non-aromatic red varieties 40% max

Colline Teramane, Montepulciano d'Abruzzo ABRUZZI, ITA Montepulciano 90% (Sangiovese 10% max)

Collio Goriziano FRIULI-VENEZIA GIULIA, ITA One or more local red varieties as a blend. The following varietal wines are also made: Cabernet Sauvignon, Cabernet Franc, Merlot, Pinot Nero

Collioure LANGUEDOC-ROUSSILLON, FRA Grenache, Mourvédre, (Carignan, Syrah, Cinsaut)

Conca de Barberá SPAIN Garnacha, *Trepat*, Tempranillo (Cabernet Sauvignon, Merlot, Pinot Noir)

Contea di Sclafani SICILY, ITA Nero d'Avola and/or *Perricone* 50% min, other local red varieties 50% max. The following varietal wines are also made: Cabernet Sauvignon, Merlot, *Perricone*, Pinot Nero, Sangiovese, Syrah

Contessa Entellina SICILY, ITA Nero d'Avola and/or Syrah, 50% min, other local non-aromatic red varieties 50% max. The following varietal wines are also made: Cabernet Sauvignon, Merlot, Pinot Nero

Controguerra ABRUZZO, ITA   Montepulciano 60% min, other local red varieties 25% max, (Merlot and/or Cabernet Sauvignon 15% min)

Copertino APULIA, ITA   Negroamaro 70-100%, (Malvasia Nera, Montepulciano, Sangiovese)

Corbières LANGUEDOC-ROUSSILLON, FRA   Carignan 40-60%, Grenache, Lladoner Pelut, Syrah, Mourvèdre, *Picpoul Noir*, *Terret Noir*, Cinsaut, (Macabéo, Bourboulenc)

Cori LATIUM, ITA   Montepulciano 40-60%, *Nero Buono di Cori* 20-40%, *Cesanese* 10-30%

Cornas RHÔNE, FRA   Syrah

Corton BURGUNDY, FRA   Pinot Noir, (Pinot Gris and Pinot Liébault allowed but virtually never used)

Cortona TUSCANY, ITA   The following varietal wines are also made: Cabernet Sauvignon, Gamay, Merlot, Pinot Nero, Sangiovese, Syrah

Costa d'Amalfi CAMPANIA, ITA   Piedirosso 40%, *Sciascinoso* and/or Aglianico 60% max, other local red varieties 40% max

Coste della Sesia PIEDMONT, ITA   Nebbiolo, Bonarda, *Vespolina*, *Croatina* and/or Barbera 50%, other local non-aromatic red varieties 50% max. The following varietal wines are also made: Bonarda, *Croatina*, Nebbiolo, *Vespolina*,

Costers del Segre SPAIN   Garnacha, Tempranillo, Cabernet Sauvignon, Merlot, Monastrell, *Trepat*, Mazuelo, Pinot Noir

Costières de Nîmes LANGUEDOC-ROUSSILLON, FRA   Carignan, Grenache, Mourvédre, Syrah, Cinsaut

Côte de Beaune BURGUNDY, FRA   Pinot Noir (Pinot Gris and Pinot Liébault allowed but virtually never used)

Côte de Beaune-Villages BURGUNDY, FRA   Pinot Noir, (Pinot Gris and Pinot Liébault allowed but virtually never used)

Côte de Brouilly BURGUNDY, FRA   Gamay, (Pinot Noir, Pinot Gris)

Côte-de-Nuits-Villages BURGUNDY, FRA   Pinot Noir, (Pinot Gris and Pinot Liébault allowed but virtually never used)

Côte Rôtie RHÔNE, FRA   Syrah 80-100% (Viognier)

Coteaux d'Aix-en-Provence PROVENCE, FRA   Grenache, Cinsaut, Syrah, Mourvèdre, Counoise, Carignan, Cabernet Sauvignon

Coteaux d'Ancenis LOIRE, FRA   Gamay, (Cabernet Sauvignon, Cabernet Franc, *Gamay de Chaudenay, Gamay de Bouze*)

Coteaux du Giennois BURGUNDY, FRA   Gamay, Pinot Noir

Coteaux du Giennois Cosne-sur-Loire BURGUNDY, FRA   Gamay, Pinot Noir

Coteaux du Languedoc LANGUEDOC-ROUSSILLON, FRA   Carignan, Grenache, Lladoner Pelut, Cinsaut, Mourvèdre, Syrah, (Counoise, *Terret Noir*, *Picpoul Noir*)

Coteaux de Loir LOIRE, FRA   Pinot d'Aunis 30% min, (Gamay, Pinot Noir, Cabernet Franc, Cabernet Sauvignon)

Coteaux du Lyonnais BURGUNDY, FRA   Gamay

Coteaux de Pierrevert RHÔNE, FRA   Carignan, Grenache, Syrah, Mourvèdre, Cinsaut, (*Terret Noir, Oeillade*)

Coteaux de Tricanstin RHÔNE, FRA   Grenache, Syrah, Mourvèdre, Cinsaut, *Picpoul Noir*, (Carignan, Grenache Blanc, Clairette, Bourbolenc, Ugni Blanc)

Coteaux de Vendômois LOIRE, FRA Pinot d'Aunis 30% min, (Gamay, Pinot Noir, Cabernet Franc, Cabernet Sauvignon)

Coteaux Varois PROVENCE, FRA Grenache, Syrah, Mourvèdre, (Carignan, Cinsaut, Cabernet Sauvignon)

Côtes Canon-Fronsac BORDEAUX, FRA Cabernet Sauvignon, Cabernet Franc, Merlot, (Malbec)

Côtes d'Auvergne LOIRE, FRA Gamay, (Pinot Noir)

Côtes de Bergerac DORDOGNE, FRA Cabernet Sauvignon, Cabernet Franc, Merlot, (Malbec, Fer, *Mérille*)

Côtes de Bourg BORDEAUX, FRA Merlot, Cabernet Sauvignon, Cabernet Franc, Malbec

Côtes du Brulhois SOUTHWEST, FRA Cabernet Sauvignon, Cabernet Franc, Merlot, Malbec, Fer, Tannnat

Côtes de Castillon BORDEAUX, FRA Merlot, Cabernet Sauvignon, Cabernet Franc, (Malbec)

Côtes de Duras SOUTHWEST, FRA Cabernet Sauvignon, Cabernet Franc, Merlot, Malbec

Côtes du Forez LOIRE, FRA Gamay

Côtes du Frontonnais HAUTE GARONNE, FRA 50-70% Négrette, (Malbec, Cabernet Sauvignon, Cabernet Franc, *Mérille*, Syrah, Fer 25% max, (Gamay, Cinsaut, Mauzac 15% max)

Côtes du Frontonnais Fronton SOUTHWEST, FRA 50-70% Négrette, (Malbec, Cabernet Sauvignon, Cabernet Franc, *Mérille*, Syrah, Fer 25% max, (Gamay, Cinsaut, Mauzac 15% max)

Côtes du Frontonnais Villaudric SOUTHWEST, FRA 50-70% Négrette, (Malbec, Cabernet Sauvignon, Cabernet Franc, *Mérille*, Syrah, Fer 25% max, (Gamay, Cinsaut, Mauzac 15% max)

Côtes du Jura JURA, FRA *Poulsard, Trousseau,* Pinot Noir

Côtes du Lubéron RHÔNE, FRA Grenache, Syrah, Mourvèdre, Cinsaut, Carignan, (*Picpoul Noir*, Pinot Noir, Counoise, Gamay)

Côtes de la Malepère LANGUEDOC-ROUSSILLON, FRA Merlot, Malbec, Cinsaut (Cabernet Sauvignon, Cabernet Franc, Grenache, Lladoner Pelut, Syrah)

Côtes du Marmandais SOUTHWEST, FRA Cabernet Sauvignon, Cabernet Franc, Merlot, (*Abouriou*, Malbec, Fer, Gamay, Syrah)

Côtes de Meliton GREECE *Athiri* 50%, Roditis 35% (Assyrtiko 15%)

Côtes de Millau LANGUEDOC-ROUSSILLON, FRA Gamay, Syrah 30% min, Fer, *Duras,* (Cabernet Sauvignon 20% max)

Côtes de Provence PROVENCE, FRA Carignan, Cinsaut, Grenache, Mourvèdre, *Tibouren*, (Syrah, Cabernet Sauvignon, *Barbaroux Rosé, Calitor,* Clairette, Sémillon, Ugni Blanc, Vermentino)

Côtes-du-Rhône RHÔNE, FRA Grenache, Clairette, Syrah, Mourvèdre, *Picpoul Noir, Terret Noir, Picardin*, Cinsaut, Roussanne, Marsanne, Bourboulenc, Viognier, Carignan, (Counoise, *Muscardin, Vaccarèse,* Pinot Blanc, Mauzac, *Pascal Blanc,* Ugni Blanc, *Camarèse, Calitor,* Gamay)

Côtes-du-Rhône-Villages RHÔNE, FRA Grenache, Cinsaut, Syrah, Mourvèdre, (Carignan, Pinot Noir, *Terret Noir,* Counoise, *Muscardin, Vaccarèse, Calitor,* Gamay)

Côtes du Roussillon LANGUEDOC-ROUSSILLON, FRA Syrah, Mourvèdre, Carignan, (Macabéo, Cinsaut, Grenache, Lladoner Pelut)

Côtes du Roussillon Villages LANGUEDOC-ROUSSILLON, FRA Syrah, Mourvèdre, Carignan, Macabéo, Cinsaut, Grenache, Lladoner Pelut

Côtes de St.-Mont SOUTHWEST, FRA Tannat, (Cabernet Sauvignon, Cabernet Franc, Merlot, Fer)

Côtes de Toul LORRAINE, FRA Pinot Noir, Pinot Meunier

Côtes du Ventoux RHÔNE, FRA Grenache, Cinsaut, Mourvèdre, Syrah, Carignan, (*Picpoul Noir*, Counoise, Clairette, Bourboulenc, Grenache Blanc, Roussanne)

Côtes du Vivarais RHÔNE, FRA Grenache, Syrah, (Cinsaut, Carignan)

Côtes Roannaises LOIRE, FRA Gamay

Crozes-Hermitage RHÔNE, FRA Syrah 85-100% (Roussanne, Marsanne)

Dão PORTUGAL Alfrocheiro, *Alvarelhão*, Aragonez, *Bastardo*, *Jaén*, *Rufete*, Tinto Cão, Touriga Nacional, Trincadeira

Dão Nobre PORTUGAL Touriga Nacional 15% min, Alfrocheiro, Aragonez, *Jaén* and/or *Rufete* 85% max

Daphnes / Dafnés GREECE *Liátiko*

Delia Nivolelli SICILY, ITA Nero d'Avola, *Perricone*, Merlot, Cabernet Sauvignon, Syrah and/or Sangiovese 65%, other local red varieties 35% max. The following varietal wines are also made: Cabernet Sauvignon, Merlot, Nero d'Avola, *Perricone*, Sangiovese, Syrah

Dingac CROATIA Plavac Mali

Dôle SWITZERLAND Pinot Noir 50% min, Gamay 50% max

Dolceacqua LIGURIA, ITA Rossese 95% min, other local non-aromatic red varieties 5% max

Dolcetto d'Acqui PIEDMONT, ITA Dolcetto

Dolcetto d'Alba PIEDMONT, ITA Dolcetto

Dolcetto d'Asti PIEDMONT, ITA Dolcetto

Dolcetto delle Langhe Monregalesi PIEDMONT, ITA Dolcetto

Dolcetto di Diano d'Alba PIEDMONT, ITA Dolcetto

Dolcetto di Dogliani PIEDMONT, ITA Dolcetto

Dolcetto di Ovada PIEDMONT, ITA Dolcetto

Donnici CALABRIA, ITA Gaglioppo 50% min, *Greco Nero* 10% min, (Malvasia, *Pecorello* and/or Greco 20% max, other local red varieties 20% max, other local white varieties 10% max)

Douro PORTUGAL Touriga National, Tinta Barroca, Tinto Cão, Tinta Roriz, Touriga Franca (Alicante Bouschet, *Alvarelhão, Alvarelhão Ceitão, Aramon*, Baga, *Barca, Barreto, Bastardo, Bragão, Camarate,* Carignan, *Carrega Tinto, Casculho, Castelã*, Castelão, *Cidadelhe, Concieira, Cornifesto, Corropio, Donzelinho Tinto, Engomada, Espadeiro, Gonçalo Pires, Grand Noir, Grangeal, Jaén, Lourela, Malandra,* Malvasia Preta, *Marufo, Melra, Mondet, Mourisco de Semente, Nevoeira, Patorra, Petit Bouschet,* Pinot Noir, *Português Azul,* Preto Martinho, *Ricoca, Roseira, Rufete, Santareno, São Saúl, Sevilhão, Sousão, Tinta Aguiar,* Tinta Barroca, *Tinta Carvalha, Tinta Fontes, Tinta Francisca, Tinta Lameira, Tinta Martins, Tinta Mesquita, Tinta Penajoia, Tinta Pereira, Tinta Pomar, Tinta Tabuaço,* Tinto Cão, *Tinto Sem Nome,* Touriga Fêmea, Trincadeira, *Valdosa, Varejoa*)

Echézeaux BURGUNDY, FRA Pinot Noir, (Pinot Gris and Pinot Liébault allowed but virtually never used)

Egri Bikavér (Bull's Blood of Eger) HUNGARY Kékfrankos, Cabernet Sauvignon, Merlot, Kékoportó, (Kadarka)

RED WINES

El Hierro SPAIN *Listán Negro, Negramoll*

Elba TUSCANY, ITA Sangiovese 75%, other local varieties 25% max

Eloro SICILY, ITA Nero d'Avola, *Pignatello* and/or Frappato 90% (other local red varieties 10% max). The following varietal wines are also made: Frappato, Nero d'Avola, *Pignatello*

Eloro Pachino SICILY, ITA Nero d'Avola 80% (Frappato and/or *Pignatello* 20% max)

Encostas De Aire PORTUGAL Castelão, Baga and/or Trincadeira 50% min, other local varieties 50% max

Esino MARCHES, ITA Sangiovese and/or Montepulciano 60%, other local red varieties 40% max

Etna SICILY, ITA Nerello Mascalese 80% min, (*Nerello Mantellato* 20% max, other local non-aromatic red varieties 10% max)

Falerno del Massico CAMPANIA, ITA Aglianico 60-80%, Piedirosso 20-40%, (Primitivo and/or Barbera 20% max)

Fara PIEDMONT, ITA Nebbiolo 30-50%, *Vespolina* 10-30%, *Bonarda Novarese* 40% max

Faro SICILY, ITA Nerello Mascalese 45-60%, *Nerello Cappuccio* 15-30%, (*Nocera* 5-10%, Nero d'Avola, Gaglioppo and/or Sangiovese 15% max)

Faros CROATIA Plavac Mali

Faugères LANGUEDOC-ROUSSILLON, FRA Carignan, Cinsaut, Syrah, Mourvèdre, Grenache, Lladoner Pelut

Fiefs Vendéens LOIRE, FRA Gamay, Pinot Noir, Cabernet Sauvignon, Cabernet Franc, Négrette, (*Gamay de Chaudenay*)

Fitou LANGUEDOC-ROUSSILLON, FRA Carignan, Grenache, Lladoner Pelut, (Mourvèdre, Syrah, Grenache Rosé, Cinsaut, Macabeo, *Terret Noir*)

Fixin BURGUNDY, FRA Pinot Noir, (Pinot Gris and Pinot Liébault allowed but virtually never used)

Fleurie BURGUNDY, FRA Gamay

Freisa d'Asti PIEDMONT, ITA Fresia

Freisa di Chieri PIEDMONT, ITA Fresia

Friuli Annia FRIULI-VENEZIA GIULIA, ITA One or more local red varieties as a blend. The following varietal wines are also made: Cabernet Sauvignon, Cabernet Franc, Merlot, Refosco

Friuli Aquileia FRIULI-VENEZIA GIULIA, ITA One or more local red varieties as a blend. The following varietal wines are also made: Cabernet Sauvignon, Cabernet Franc, Merlot, Refosco

Friuli Grave FRIULI-VENEZIA GIULIA, ITA One or more local non-aromatic red varieties as a blend. The following varietal wines are also made: Cabernet Sauvignon, Cabernet Franc, Franconia, Merlot, Pinot Nero, Refosco

Friuli Isonzo FRIULI-VENEZIA GIULIA, ITA One or more local non-aromatic red varieties as a blend. The following varietal wines are also made: Cabernet Sauvignon, Cabernet Franc, Merlot, Pinot Nero, Refosco, Schioppettino

Friuli Latisana FRIULI-VENEZIA GIULIA, ITA The following varietal wines are also made: Cabernet Sauvignon, Cabernet Franc, Merlot, Pinot Nero, Refosco

Fronsac BORDEAUX, FRA Cabernet Sauvignon, Cabernet Franc, Merlot, (Malbec)

Gabiano PIEDMONT, ITA Barbera 90-95% (Freisa and/or Grignolino 10% max)

Gaillac SOUTHWEST, FRA *Duras*, Fer, Syrah 60% min, (Cabernet Sauvignon, Cabernet Franc, Gamay, Merlot)

Galantina APULIA, ITA Negroamaro 65% min, non-aromatic local red varieties 35% max

Gallucio CAMPANIA, ITA Aglianico 70% min, other local red varieties 30% max

Garda LOMBARDY & VENETO, ITA The following varietal wines are also made: Barbera, Cabernet Sauvignon, Cabernet Franc, Corvina, *Groppello*, Marzemino, Merlot, Pinot Nero

Garda Colli Mantovani LOMBARDY, ITA Cabernet Franc and/or Cabernet Sauvignon 20-50%, Merlot 20-40%, Rondinella 20-30%, (Sangiovese, Molinara and/or *Negrara Trentina* 15% max). The following varietal wines are also made: Cabernet Franc, Cabernet Sauvignon, Merlot

Gattinara PIEDMONT, ITA Nebbiolo 90%-100%, (*Bonarda di Gattinara* max 10%, *Vespolina* max 4%)

Genazzano LATIUM, ITA Sangiovese 70-90%, *Cesanese Comune* 10-30% (other local red varieties 20% max)

Gevrey-Chambertin BURGUNDY, FRA Pinot Noir, (Pinot Gris and Pinot Liébault allowed but virtually never used)

Ghemme PIEDMONT, ITA Nebbiolo 65-85%, (*Vespolina* 10-30%, *Bonarda Novarese* 15%)

Gigondas RHÔNE, FRA Grenache 60%-75%, Syrah, Mourvèdre, (*Terret Noir*, Counoise, *Muscardin*, *Vaccarèse*, *Calitor*, Gamay, Cinsaut)

Gioia del Colle APULIA, ITA Primitivo 50-60%, Montepulciano, Sangiovese, Negroamaro and/or Malvasia Nera 40-50%. The following varietal wines are also made: Aleatico, Primitivo

Girò di Cagliari SARDINIA, ITA *Girò*

Givry BURGUNDY, FRA Pinot Noir, (Pinot Gris and Pinot Liébault allowed but virtually never used)

Golfo del Tigullio LIGURIA, ITA *Ciliegiolo* 20-70%, Dolcetto 20-70%, other local non-aromatic red varieties 40% max. The following varietal wine is also made: *Ciliegiolo*

Goron SWITZERLAND Pinot Noir, Gamay

Gouménissa GREECE Xynómavro, (*Negóska* 20% min)

Grands Echézeaux BURGUNDY, FRA Pinot Noir, (Pinot Gris and Pinot Liébault allowed but virtually never used)

Graves BORDEAUX, FRA Cabernet Sauvignon, Cabernet Franc, Merlot, (Petit Verdot)

Graves de Vayres BORDEAUX, FRA Cabernet Sauvignon, Cabernet Franc, Merlot, (Malbec, Petit Verdot)

Grignolino d'Asti PIEDMONT, ITA Grignolino 90% min (Freisa 10% max)

Grignolino del Monferrato Casalese PIEDMONT, ITA Grignolino 90% min, (Freisa 10% max)

Griottes-Chambertin BURGUNDY, FRA Pinot Noir, (Pinot Gris and Pinot Liébault allowed but virtually never used)

Guardia Sanframondi CAMPANIA, ITA Sangiovese 80% min, other local red varieties 20% max

Guardiolo CAMPANIA, ITA Sangiovese 80% min, other local red varieties 20% max

Gutariako Txacoli SPAIN *Hondarrabi Beltza*

Haut-Médoc BORDEAUX, FRA Cabernet Sauvignon, Cabernet Franc, Merlot, (Carmenère, Malbec, Petit Verdot)

Haut-Poitou LOIRE, FRA Cabernet Franc, Cabernet Sauvignon, Gamay, Merlot, Malbec, (Grolleau, *Gamay de Chaudenay*)

Hermitage RHÔNE, FRA Syrah 85-100%, (Roussanne, Marsanne)

Irouléguy SOUTHWEST, FRA Tannat, Cabernet Sauvignon, Cabernet Franc

Ischia CAMPANIA, ITA Grenache 40-50%, Piedirosso 40-50%, other local red varieties 15% max

Jasnières LOIRE, FRA Gamay, Pinot d'Aunis

Juliénas BURGUNDY, FRA Gamay

Jumilla SPAIN Monastrell, (Garnacha Tintorera, Tempranillo, Garnacha, Cabernet Sauvignon)

Jumilla-Monastrell SPAIN Monastrell 85% min, (Garnacha Tintorera, Tempranillo, Garnacha, Cabernet Sauvignon)

La Grande Rue BURGUNDY, FRA Pinot Noir, (Pinot Gris and Pinot Liébault allowed but virtually never used)

La Mancha SPAIN Tempranillo, *Moravia*, Garnacha, Cabernet Sauvignon

La Palma SPAIN *Negramoll*, (*Listán Negro, Malvasía Rosada, Moscatel Negro, Tintilla*)

La Romanée BURGUNDY, FRA Pinot Noir, (Pinot Gris and Pinot Liébault allowed but virtually never used)

La Tâche BURGUNDY, FRA Pinot Noir, (Pinot Gris and Pinot Liébault allowed but virtually never used)

Lacrima di Morro d'Alba MARCHES, ITA Lacrima 85% min, (Montepulciano and/or Verdicchio 15% max)

Lacryma Christi del Vesuvio CAMPANIA, ITA Piedirosso and/or *Sciascinoso* 80%, (Aglianico 20% max)

Ladoix BURGUNDY, FRA Pinot Noir, (Pinot Gris and Pinot Liébault allowed but virtually never used)

Lafões PORTUGAL Amaral 40% min, *Jaén, Pilongo*

Lago di Caldaro TRENTINO-ALTO ADIGE, ITA Schiava 85-100% (Pinot Nero and/or Lagrein 15% max)

Lago di Corbara UMBRIA, ITA Cabernet Sauvignon, Merlot, Pinot Nero and/or Sangiovese 70% min, Aleatico, Barbera, Cabernet Franc, Canaiolo, *Cesanese, Ciliegiolo, Colorino*, Dolcetto and/or Montepulciano 30% max. The following varietal wines are also made: Cabernet Sauvignon, Merlot, Pinot Nero

Lagoa PORTUGAL Negra Mole and/or Trincadeira 70% min, Alicante Bouschet, Aragonez, Cabernet Sauvignon, Castelão, *Monvedro, Moreto*, Syrah, Touriga Franca and/or Touriga Nacional 30% min

Lagos PORTUGAL Castelão, Negra Mole and/or Trincadeira 70% min, Alicante Bouschet, Aragonez, *Bastardo*, Cabernet Sauvignon, *Monvedro* and/or Touriga Nacional 30% max

Lalande-de-Pomerol BORDEAUX, FRA Merlot, (Cabernet Franc, Cabernet Sauvignon, Malbec)

Lambrusco di Sorbara EMILIA-ROMAGNA, ITA Lambrusco di Sorbara 60% min, Lambrusco Salamino 40% max

Lambrusco Grasparossa di Castelvetro EMILIA-ROMAGNA, ITA
Lambrusco Grasparossa 85% min, (other Lambrusco varieties, *Fortana*,
Malbo Gentile 15% max)

Lambrusco Mantovano EMILIA-ROMAGNA, ITA Lambrusco Viadanese,
Lambrusco Maestri, Lambrusco Marani and/or Lambrusco Salamino
85% min, (Lambrusco di Sorbara, Lambrusco Grasparossa, *Ancellotta*,
Fortana 15%)

Lambrusco Salamino di Santa Croce EMILIA-ROMAGNA, ITA Lambrusco
Salamino 90% min, (other Lambrusco varieties, *Ancellotta* and/or
Fortana 10% max)

Lamezia CALABRIA, ITA Nerello Mascalese and/or *Nerello Cappuccio*
30-50%, Gaglioppo and/or *Magliocco* 25-35%, *Greco Nero* and/or
Marsigliana 25-35%, (other local red varieties 20% max)

Langhe PIEDMONT, ITA One or more local non-aromatic red varieties.
The following varietal wines are also made: Dolcetto, Freisa, Nebbiolo

Lanzarote SPAIN *Listán Negra, Negramoll*

Latricières-Chambertin BURGUNDY, FRA Pinot Noir, (Pinot Gris and
Pinot Liébault allowed but virtually never used)

Les Baux de Provence PROVENCE, FRA Grenache, Cinsaut, Syrah,
(Mourvèdre, Counise, Carignan, Cabernet Sauvignon)

Lessona PIEDMONT, ITA Nebbiolo 75% min (Bonarda and/or *Vespolina*
25% max)

Leverano APULIA, ITA Negroamaro 50% min, Montepulciano,
Sangiovese and/or *Malvasia Nera* 40% max, other local red varieties
30% max

Lirac RHÔNE, FRA Grenache 40% min, Syrah, Mourvèdre, Cinsaut,
(Carignan)

Lison-Pramaggiore VENETO/FRIULI-VENEZIA GIULIA, ITA Merlot 50-
70%, other local non-aromatic red varieties 50% max. The following
varietal wines are also made: Cabernet Franc, Cabernet Sauvignon,
Malbec, Merlot, Refosco

Listrac-Médoc BORDEAUX, FRA Cabernet Sauvignon, Cabernet Franc,
Merlot, (Carmenère, Malbec, Petit Verdot)

Lizzano APULIA, ITA Negroamaro 60-80%, Montepulciano, Sangiovese,
Bombino Nero and/or Pinot Nero 40% max, (other local red varieties
10% max)

Lussac-St-Émilion BORDEAUX, FRA Merlot, (Cabernet Franc, Cabernet
Sauvignon, Malbec)

**Mâcon or Mâcon followed by village name (ie Mâcon-Burgy, Mâcon-
Chardonnay, etc)** BURGUNDY, FRA Gamay, Pinot Noir, Pinot Gris

Mâcon Supérieur BURGUNDY, FRA Gamay, Pinot Noir, Pinot Gris

Madiran SOUTHWEST, FRA Tannat 40-100%, Cabernet Franc, (Cabernet
Sauvignon, Fer)

Manchuela SPAIN Bobal, (Tempranillo, Cabernet Sauvignon, Garnacha,
Merlot, Syrah, Monastrell, *Moravia*)

Mandrolisai SARDINIA, ITA *Bovale Sardo* 35% min, Grenache 20-35%,
Monica 20-35%, (other local red varieties 10% max)

Maranges BURGUNDY, FRA Pinot Noir, (Pinot Gris and Pinot Liébault
allowed but virtually never used)

Marcillac SOUTHWEST, FRA Fer 90% Min, (Cabernet Franc, Cabernet
Sauvignon, Merlot)

Margaux BORDEAUX, FRA Cabernet Sauvignon, Cabernet Franc, Merlot, (Carmenère, Malbec, Petit Verdot)

Marsannay BURGUNDY, FRA Pinot Noir, (Pinot Gris and Pinot Liébault allowed but virtually never used)

Matino APULIA, ITA Negroamaro, (Sangiovese, Malvasia Nera 35% max)

Mazis-Chambertin BURGUNDY, FRA Pinot Noir, (Pinot Gris and Pinot Liébault allowed but virtually never used)

Mazoyères-Chambertin BURGUNDY, FRA Pinot Noir, (Pinot Gris and Pinot Liébault allowed but virtually never used)

Médoc BORDEAUX, FRA Cabernet Sauvignon, Cabernet Franc, Merlot, (Carmenère, Malbec, Petit Verdot)

Melissa CALABRIA, ITA Gaglioppo, 75-95%, *Greco Nero*, Greco, Trebbiano, Malvasia 5-25% max

Menetou-Salon LOIRE, FRA Pinot Noir

Menfi SICILY, ITA Nero d'Avola, Sangiovese, Merlot, Cabernet Sauvignon and/or Syrah 70%, other local red varieties 30% max. The following varietal wines are also made: Cabernet Sauvignon, Merlot, Nero d'Avola, Sangiovese, Syrah

Méntrida SPAIN Garnacha, (*Tinto Basto*, Tempranillo, Cabernet Sauvignon)

Mercurey BURGUNDY, FRA Pinot Noir, (Pinot Gris and Pinot Liébault allowed but virtually never used)

Merlara VENETO, ITA Merlot 50-70%, other local non-aromatic red varieties 50% max. The following varietal wines are also made: Cabernet Sauvignon, Merlot

Messenikóla GREECE *Mavro Messenikola* 70%, Carignane and Syrah 30%

Meursault BURGUNDY, FRA Pinot Noir, (Pinot Gris and Pinot Liébault allowed but virtually never used)

Minervois LANGUEDOC-ROUSSILLON, FRA Carignan, Grenache, Lladoner Pelut, Mourvèdre, Syrah, (Cinsaut, *Aspiran Noir, Terret Noir, Picpoul Noir*)

Molise MOLISE, ITA Montepulciano (other local non-aromatic red varieties 15% max). The following varietal wines are also made: Aglianico, Cabernet Sauvignon, Sangiovese, *Tintilia*

Mondéjar SPAIN Tempranillo, Cabernet Sauvignon (*Tinto de Madrid*, Garnacha, *Jaén*)

Monferrato PIEDMONT, ITA One or more local non-aromatic red varieties. The following varietal wines are also made: Dolcetto, Freisa

Monica di Cagliari SARDINIA, ITA Monica

Monica di Sardegna SARDINIA, ITA Monica 85% min, other local red varieties 15% max

Monreale SICILY, ITA Calabrese/Nero d'Avola and *Perricone* 50%, other local red varieties 50% max. The following varietal wines are also made: Cabernet Sauvignon, Calabrese, Merlot, *Perricone*, Pinot Nero, Sangiovese, Syrah

Montagne-St-Émilion BORDEAUX, FRA Merlot, (Cabernet Franc, Cabernet Sauvignon, Malbec)

Montecarlo TUSCANY, ITA Sangiovese 50-75%, (Canaiolo Nero 5-15%, *Ciliegiolo, Colorino*, Malvasia Nera, Syrah, Cabernet Franc, Cabernet Sauvignon and/or Merlot 10-15%)

Montecucco TUSCANY, ITA Sangiovese 60% min, other local non-aromatic red varieties 40% max. The following varietal wine is also made: Sangiovese

Montefalco UMBRIA, ITA Sangiovese 60-70%, other local non-aromatic red varieties 30% max, (Sagrantino 10-15% max)

Montefalco Sagrantino UMBRIA, ITA Sagrantino 100% max, (Trebbiano Toscano 5% max)

Montello e Colli Asolani VENETO, ITA Merlot 40-60%, Cabernet Franc 20-30%, Cabernet Sauvignon 10-20%, (other local red varieties 15% max). The following varietal wines are also made: Cabernet Franc, Cabernet Sauvignon, Merlot

Montepulciano d'Abruzzo ABRUZZI, ITA Montepulciano 85% (other local red varieties 15% max)

Monteregio di Massa Marittima TUSCANY, ITA Sangiovese 80% min (other local red varieties 20% max)

Monterrei SPAIN *Mencía* and/or *Merenzao* 65% min (*Alicante*, *Gran Negro*, Tempranillo, Cabernet Sauvignon, *Mouratón*)

Monterrei Superior SPAIN *Mencía* and/or *Merenzao* 85% min (*Alicante*, *Gran Negro*, Tempranillo, Cabernet Sauvignon, *Mouratón*)

Montescudaio TUSCANY, ITA Sangiovese 50% min, other local red varieties 50% max. The following varietal wines are also made: Cabernet Franc, Cabernet Sauvignon, Merlot, Sangiovese

Monthélie BURGUNDY, FRA Pinot Noir, (Pinot Gris and Pinot Liébault allowed but virtually never used)

Monti Lessini VENETO, ITA Merlot 50% min, Pinot Nero, Corvina, Cabernet Franc, Cabernet Sauvignon and/or Carmenère 50% max

Morellino di Scansano TUSCANY, ITA Sangiovese 85% min, (other local red varieties 15% max)

Morey St.-Denis BURGUNDY, FRA Pinot Noir, (Pinot Gris and Pinot Liébault allowed but virtually never used)

Morgon BURGUNDY, FRA Gamay

Moulin-à-Vent BURGUNDY, FRA Gamay

Moulis BORDEAUX, FRA Cabernet Sauvignon, Cabernet Franc, Merlot, (Carmenère, Malbec, Petit Verdot)

Musigny BURGUNDY, FRA Pinot Noir, (Pinot Gris and Pinot Liébault allowed but virtually never used)

Náousa GREECE Xynómavro

Nardò APULIA, ITA Negroamaro 80% min (Montepulciano and/or Malvasia Nera 20% max)

Navarra SPAIN Garnacha, Tempranillo, Merlot, Cabernet Sauvignon, Graciano, Mazuelo

Néac BORDEAUX, FRA Merlot, (Cabernet Franc, Cabernet Sauvignon, Malbec)

Nebbiolo d'Alba PIEDMONT, ITA Nebbiolo

Neméa (Blood of Hercules) GREECE Agiorgitiko

Nuits-St.-Georges BURGUNDY, FRA Pinot Noir, (Pinot Gris and Pinot Liébault allowed but virtually never used)

Óbidos PORTUGAL Aragonez, Castelão and/or Touriga Nacional 65% min, Syrah, *Tinta Miúda* and/or Touriga Franca 35% max, (Alicante Bouschet and/or *Caladoc* 15% max)

Offida MARCHES, ITA Montepulciano 50%, Cabernet Sauvignon 30% (other local non-aromatic red varieties 20% max)

Oltrepo Pavese LOMBARDY, ITA Barbera 25-65%, *Croatina* 25-65%, *Uva Rara, Ughetta* and/or Pinot Nero 45% max. The following varietal wines are also made: Barbera, Bonarda, *Buttafuoco*, Cabernet Sauvignon, Pinot Nero, *Sangue di Giuda*

Orcia TUSCANY, ITA Sangiovese 60%, other local non-aromatic varieties 40% max (white varieties 10% max)

Orta Nova APULIA, ITA Sangiovese 60%, Uva di Troia, and/or Montepulciano 30-40%, (Lambrusco Maestri and/or Trebbiano Toscano 10% max)

Ostuni Ottavianello APULIA, ITA Cinsaut 85% min (Negroamaro, Malvasia Nera, *Notar Domenico* and/or *Sussumaniello* 15% max)

Palette PROVENCE, FRA Grenache, Cinsaut, Mourvèdre, (*Téoulier, Durif,* Syrah, Carignan, Cabernet Sauvignon, Muscat, *Castets, Brun-Fourcat, Terret Gris, Petit-Brun, Tibouren,* Clairette, *Picardan,* Ugni Blanc, *Ugni Rosé,* Grenache Blanc, Picpoul, *Pascal, Aragnan,* Colombard, *Terret-Bourret*)

Palmela PORTUGAL Castelão 67% min, Alfrocheiro, *Bastardo*, Cabernet Sauvignon and/or Trincadeira 33% max

Páros GREECE *Mandilariá* 66%, *Monemvasiá* 33%. The following varietal wine is also made: *Monemvasiá*

Parrina TUSCANY, ITA Sangiovese 70% min, other local red varieties 30% max

Parsac-St-Émilion BORDEAUX, FRA Merlot, (Cabernet Franc, Cabernet Sauvignon, Malbec)

Patrimonio CORSICA, FRA *Nielluccio* 90% min, (Grenache, *Sciacarello,* Vermentino)

Pauillac BORDEAUX, FRA Cabernet Sauvignon, Cabernet Franc, Merlot, (Carmenère, Malbec, Petit Verdot)

Pécharmant SOUTHWEST, FRA Cabernet Franc, Cabernet Sauvignon, Merlot

Pelješac CROATIA Plavac Mali

Penedés SPAIN Garnacha, Cariñena, Tempranillo, *Samsó,* Monastrell, Cabernet Sauvignon (Cabernet Franc, Merlot, Pinot Noir)

Penisola Sorrentina CAMPANIA, ITA Piedirosso, *Sciascinoso* and/or Aglianico 60%, other local red varieties 40% max

Pentro di Isernia MOLISE, ITA Montepulciano 45-55%, Sangiovese 45-55%, (other local red varieties 10% max)

Pernard-Vergelesses BURGUNDY, FRA Pinot Noir, (Pinot Gris and Pinot Liébault allowed but virtually never used)

Pessac-Léognan BORDEAUX, FRA Cabernet Sauvignon, Cabernet Franc, Merlot, (Carmenère, Malbec, Petit Verdot)

Pezá GREECE *Kotsifáli, Mandylariá*

Piave VENETO, ITA The following varietal wines are made: Cabernet Franc, Cabernet Sauvignon, Merlot, Pinot Nero, Raboso

Pic-St.-Loup, Coteaux du Languedoc LANGUEDOC-ROUSSILLON, FRA Grenache, Mourvèdre, Syrah, (Carignan, Cinsaut)

Piemonte PIEDMONT, ITA The following varietal wines are made: Barbera, Bonarda, Brachetto, Grignolino

RED WINES

Pinerolese PIEDMONT, ITA Barbera, Bonarda, Nebbiolo and/or *Neretto* 50% min, other local non-aromatic red varieties 50% max. The following varietal wines are also made: Barbera, Bonarda, Brachetto, Dolcetto, *Doux d'Henry,* Freisa

Pinerolese Rami'e PIEDMONT, ITA *Avanà* 30%, other local non-aromatic red varieties 35% max, (*Avarengo* 15%, *Neretto* 20%)

Pla de Bagés SPAIN Tempranillo, Garnacha, Merlot, Cabernet Sauvignon, (Syrah)

Pla i llevant SPAIN *Callet*, Tempranillo, *Manto Negro*, Cabernet Sauvignon, (Monastrell, Syrah, Pinot Noir)

Planalto Mirandês PORTUGAL *Bastardo*, *Marufo*, Trincadeira, Touriga Franca and/or Touriga Nacional 60% min, other local varieties 40% max

Pollino CALABRIA, ITA Gaglioppo 60% min, (*Greco Nero*, Malvasia, *Montonico Bianco* and/or *Guarnaccia Bianca* 20%, other local white varieties 20% max)

Pomerol BORDEAUX, FRA Merlot, (Cabernet Franc, Cabernet Sauvignon, Malbec)

> **Pétrus**, a famous Pomerol, has vineyards comprising 95% Merlot and 5% Cabernet Franc.

Pomino TUSCANY, ITA Sangiovese 60-70%, Canaiolo, Cabernet Sauvignon and/or Cabernet franc 15-25%, (Merlot 10-20%, other local red varieties 15% max)

Pommard BURGUNDY, FRA Pinot Noir, (Pinot Gris and Pinot Liébault allowed but virtually never used)

Portimão PORTUGAL Castelão, Negra Mole and/or Trincadeira 70% min, Alicante Bouschet, Aragonez, Cabernet Sauvignon, *Monvedro*, Syrah and/or Touriga Nacional 30% max

Postup CROATIA Plavac Mali

Potomje CROATIA Plavac Mali

Premières Côtes de Blaye BORDEAUX, FRA Cabernet Sauvignon, Cabernet Franc, Merlot, (Malbec)

Premières Côtes de Bordeaux BORDEAUX, FRA Cabernet Sauvignon, Cabernet Franc, Merlot, (Carmenère, Malbec, Petit Verdot)

Primitivo di Manduria PUGLIA, ITA Primitivo

Priorato SPAIN Garnacha, (Garnacha Peluda, Cariñena, Cabernet Sauvignon)

Prošek CROATIA Plavac Mali

Puisseguin-St-Émilion BORDEAUX, FRA Merlot, (Cabernet Franc, Cabernet Sauvignon, Malbec)

Puligny-Montrachet BURGUNDY, FRA Pinot Noir, (Pinot Gris and Pinot Liébault allowed but virtually never used)

Rapsani GREECE *Krasáto*, *Stavrotó*, Xynómavro

Reggiano EMILIA-ROMAGNA, ITA Lambrusco Marani, Lambrusco Salamino, Lambrusco Montericco, Lambrusco Maestri and/or Lambrusco di Sorbara 85%, (*Ancellotta* and/or *Malbo Gentile* 15% max)

Régnié BURGUNDY, FRA Gamay

RED WINES

Reuilly LOIRE, FRA Pinot Noir, Pinot Gris

Rhodes / Ródos GREECE *Mandilaría*

Rías Baixas SPAIN *Caiño Tinto, Sousón, Espadeiro, Brancella, Mencí, Loureiro Tinto*

Ribatejo PORTUGAL Aragonez, Baga, *Camarate*, Castelão, *Preto Martinho, Tinta Miúda*, Touriga Franca, Touriga Nacional and/or Trincadeira 50% min, Alfrocheiro, Alicante Bouchet, *Bastardo*, Cabernet Sauvignon, *Caladoc, Esgana Cão Tinto, Grand Noir, Jaén*, Merlot, *Moreto*, Petit Verdot, Pinot Noir, Tinta Barroca, *Tinta Caiada* and/or Tinto Cão 50% max

Ribeira Sacra SPAIN *Mencía, Brancellao, Merenzao, Caiño, Sousón, Espadeiro*

Ribeiro SPAIN *Caiño, · Ferrón, Sousón, Brancellao, (Mencía,* Tempranillo, Garnacha Tintorera)

Ribeiro del Duero SPAIN Tempranillo 75% min, Cabernet Sauvignon, Merlot and/or Malbec 0-25%, (Garnacha 5% max)

Ribera del Guadiana SPAIN Tempranillo, Garnacha, Bobal, Cabernet Sauvignon, Graciano, Mazuelo, Merlot, Monastrell, Syrah

Richebourg BURGUNDY, FRA Pinot Noir, (Pinot Gris and Pinot Liébault allowed but virtually never used)

Rioja SPAIN Tempranillo, Garnacha, Graciano, Carignan

> **Marquès de Murrieta Castillo Ygay**, a traditional Rioja, was 75% Tempranillo, 10% Garnacha, 13% Carignan and 2% Graciano in the 1994 vintage.

Riviera del Garda Bresciano LOMBARDY, ITA *Groppello Gentile, Mocasina, S.Stefano* and/or Sangiovese 30-60%, (Barbera 10-20%, Marzemino 5-30%, other local red varieties 10% max)

Riviera Ligure di Ponente LIGURIA, ITA The following varietal wines are made: *Ormeasco, Rossese*

Roero PIEDMONT, ITA Nebbiolo 95% (Arneis 2-5%, other local varieties 3% max)

Romanée-Conti BURGUNDY, FRA Pinot Noir, (Pinot Gris and Pinot Liébault allowed but virtually never used)

Romanée-St-Vivant BURGUNDY, FRA Pinot Noir, (Pinot Gris and Pinot Liébault allowed but virtually never used)

Rosso Barletta APULIA, ITA Uva di Troia 70% min, Sangiovese and/or Montepulciano 30% max, (Malbec 10% max)

Rosso Canosa APULIA, ITA Uva di Troia 65% min, Sangiovese and/or Montepulciano 35% max (other local red varieties 5% max)

Rosso Canisium APULIA, ITA Uva di Troia 65% min, Sangiovese and/or Montepulciano 35% max (other local red varieties, 5% max)

Rosso Conero MARCHES, ITA Montepulciano 85% min, Sangiovese 15% max

Rosso di Cerignola APULIA, ITA Uva di Troia 55% min, Negroamaro 15-30% (Sangiovese, Barbera, Malvasia, Trebbiano and/or Montepulciano 15% max)

Rosso di Montalcino TUSCANY, ITA Sangiovese

Rosso di Montepulciano TUSCANY, ITA Sangiovese 70% (Canaiolo 20%

RED WINES

max, other local varieties - with the exception of all aromatic types but Malvasia del Chianti -20% max, local white varieties 10% max)

Rosso Orvietano UMBRIA, ITA Aleatico, Cabernet Franc, Cabernet Sauvignon, Canaiolo, *Ciliegiolo*, Merlot, Montepulciano, Pinot Nero and/or Sangiovese 70% min (Barbera, *Cesanese Comune, Colorino* and/or Dolcetto 30% max). The following varietal wines are also made: Aleatico, Cabernet Franc, Cabernet Sauvignon, Canaiolo, *Ciliegiolo*, Merlot, Pinot Nero, Sangiovese

Rosso Piceno MARCHES, ITA Montepulciano 35-70%, Sangiovese, 30-50% (other local non-aromatic red varieties 15% max)

Rubino di Cantavenna PIEDMONT, ITA Barbera 75-90%, Grignolino and/or Freisa 25% max

Ruché di Castagnole Monferrato PIEDMONT, ITA Ruché 90% min (Barbera and/or Brachetto 10% max)

Ruchottes-Chambertin BURGUNDY, FRA Pinot Noir, (Pinot Gris and Pinot Liébault allowed but virtually never used)

Rully BURGUNDY, FRA Pinot Noir, (Pinot Gris and Pinot Liébault allowed but virtually never used)

St.-Aubin BURGUNDY, FRA Pinot Noir, (Pinot Gris and Pinot Liébault allowed but virtually never used)

St.-Amour BURGUNDY, FRA Gamay

St.-Chinian LANGUEDOC-ROUSSILLON, FRA Carignan, Cinsaut, Grenache, Mourvèdre, Syrah, Lladoner Pelut

St.-Émilion BORDEAUX, FRA Merlot, Cabernet Franc, Cabernet Sauvignon, (Malbec, Carmenère)

> **Château Cheval Blanc**, a very famous St.-Émilion, has vineyards comprising 60% Cabernet Franc, 34% Merlot, 5% Malbec and 1% Cabernet Sauvignon.

St.-Estèphe BORDEAUX, FRA Cabernet Sauvignon, Merlot, Cabernet Franc, (Malbec, Carmenère, Petit Verdot)

Ste.-Foy-Bordeaux BORDEAUX, FRA Cabernet Sauvignon, Cabernet Franc, Malbec, (Petite Verdot)

St-Georges-St-Émilion BORDEAUX, FRA Merlot, (Cabernet Franc, Cabernet Sauvignon, Malbec)

St.-Joseph RHÔNE, FRA Syrah 90-100%, Marsanne, Roussanne

St.-Julien BORDEAUX, FRA Cabernet Sauvignon, Cabernet Franc, Merlot, (Carmenère, Malbec, Petit Verdot)

St.-Nicolas-de-Bourgueil LOIRE, FRA Cabernet Franc 90-100%, (Cabernet Sauvignon)

Saint-Pourçain LOIRE, FRA Gamay, Pinot Noir, (Gamay Teinturier)

St.-Romain BURGUNDY, FRA Pinot Noir, (Pinot Gris and Pinot Liébault allowed but virtually never used)

Salice Salentino APULIA, ITA Negroamaro 80% min (Malvasia Nera 20% max)

Sambuca di Sicilia SICILY, ITA Nero d'Avola 50-100%, other local non-aromatic varieties 50% max. The following varietal wines are also made: Cabernet Sauvignon, Merlot, Nero d'Avola, Sangiovese, Syrah

Sancerre LOIRE, FRA Pinot Noir

San Colombano al Lambro LOMBARDY, ITA *Croatina* 30-45%, Barbera 25-50%, (*Uva Rara* 5-15%, other local red varieties 15% max)

San Gimignano TUSCANY, ITA Sangiovese 50%, other local red varieties 50% max

Sangiovese di Romagna EMILIA-ROMAGNA, ITA Sangiovese

Sannio CAMPANIA, ITA Sangiovese 50% min, other local red varieties 50% max. The following varietal wines are also made: Aglianico, Barbera, Piedirosso

San Severo APULIA, ITA Montepulciano 70% min, Sangiovese

San Vito di Luzzi CALABRIA, ITA Gaglioppo 70% min, *Greco Nero*, Sangiovese and/or other local red varieties 30% max, (Malvasia 10% max)

Sant'Agata dei Goti CALABRIA, ITA Aglianico 40-60%, Piedirosso 40-60%, (other local red varieties 20% max)

Sant'Anna di Isola Capo Rizzuto CALABRIA, ITA Gaglioppo 40-60%, *Nocera*, Nerello Mascalese, *Nerello Cappuccio*, Malvasia Nera, Malvasia and/or Greco 40-60% with the white grape varieties limited to 35%

Sant'Antimo TUSCANY, ITA One or more local red varieties. The following varietal wines are also made: Cabernet Sauvignon, Merlot, Pinot Nero

Santa Margherita di Belice SICILY, ITA Nero d'Avola 20-50%, Sangiovese and/or Cabernet Sauvignon 50-80%, (other local red varieties 15% max). The following varietal wines are also made: Nero d'Avola, Sangiovese

Santenay BURGUNDY, FRA Pinot Noir, (Pinot Gris and Pinot Liébault allowed but virtually never used)

Sassicaia, Bolgheri TUSCANY, ITA Cabernet Sauvignon 80%, (other local red varieties 20% max)

Saumur LOIRE, FRA Cabernet Franc, (Cabernet Sauvignon, Pineau d'Aunis)

Saumur-Champigny LOIRE, FRA Cabernet Franc, (Cabernet Sauvignon, Pineau d'Aunis)

Savigny-lès-Beaune BURGUNDY, FRA Pinot Noir, (Pinot Gris and Pinot Liébault allowed but virtually never used)

Savuto CALABRIA, ITA Gaglioppo 35-45%, Greco Nero, *Nerello Cappuccio, Magliocco Ganino* and/or Sangiovese 30-40%, Malvasia and/or *Pecorino* 25% max

Scavigna CALABRIA, ITA Gaglioppo 60% max, *Nerello Cappuccio* 40% max, other local red varieties 40% max

Sciacca SICILY, ITA Merlot, Cabernet Sauvignon, Nero d'Avola and/or Sangiovese 70%, other local non-aromatic red varieties 30% max. The following varietal wines are also made: Cabernet Sauvignon, Merlot, Nero d'Avola, Sangiovese

Sforzato di Valtellina / Sfursat di Valtellina LOMBARDY, ITA Nebbiolo 90-100%, (other local red varieties 10%max)

Sitía GREECE *Liátiko* 80%, (*Mandilariá* 20%)

Sizzano PIEDMONT, ITA Nebbiolo 40-60%, *Vespolina* 15-40%, *Bonarda Novarese* 25% max. The following varietal wine is also made: Sangiovese

Solopaca CALABRIA, ITA Sangiovese 50-60%, Aglianico 20-40%, Piedirosso, *Sciascinoso* and/or other local red varieties 30% max. The following varietal wine is also made: Aglianico

Somontano SPAIN *Moristel,* Tempranillo, Garnacha, *Parreleta,* Cabernet Sauvignon

Sovana CALABRIA, ITA Sangiovese 50%, other local non-aromatic red varieties 50% max. The following varietal wines are also made: Aleatico, Cabernet Sauvignon, Merlot, Sangiovese

Squinzano APULIA, ITA Negroamaro 70% min (Sangiovese and/or Malvasia Nera 30% max)

Südtirol Bozner Leiten ALTO ADIGE, ITA Schiava 90% min, (Lagrein, Pinot Nero)

Südtirol Kalterersee ALTO ADIGE, ITA Schiava 85% min, (Lagrein, Pinot Nero)

Südtirol Meraner ALTO ADIGE, ITA Schiava

Südtirol St. Magdalener ALTO ADIGE, ITA Schiava 90% min, (Lagrein, Pinot Nero)

Taburno CAMPANIA, ITA Sangiovese, 40-50%, Aglianico 30-40%, other local red varieties 30% max. The following varietal wine is also made: Piedirosso

Taburno Novello CAMPANIA, ITA Aglianico 85% min, (other local red varieties 15% max)

Tacoronte-Acentejo SPAIN *Listán Negro, Negramol*

Tarquinia LATIUM, ITA Sangiovese and/or Montepulciano, 60%, *Cesanese Comune* 25% max, other local red varieties 30% max

Tarragona SPAIN Mazuelo, Garnacha, Tempranillo

Taurasi CAMPANIA, ITA Aglianico 85% min, (local red varieties)

Tavira PORTUGAL Castelão, Negra Mole and/or Trincadeira 70% min, Alicante Bouschet, Aragonez, Cabernet Sauvignon, Syrah and/or Touriga Nacional 30% max

Távora-Varosa PORTUGAL *Alvarelhão,* Aragonez, *Bastardo,* Castelão, Malvasia Preta, *Marufo, Rufete,* Tinta Barroca, *Barca,* Touriga Franca, Touriga Nacional, *Vinhão*

Teroldego Rotaliano TRENTINO-ALTO ADIGE, ITA Teroldego

Terra Alta SPAIN Mazuelo, Garnacha, Garnacha Peluda, Cabernet Sauvignon, Merlot, Tempranillo

Terralba SARDINIA, ITA *Bovale di Spagna* and/or *Bovale Sardo* 80%, *Pascale di Cagliari,* (Greco and/or Monica 20% max)

Terre di Franciacorta LOMBARDY, ITA Cabernet Sauvignon, Cabernet Franc 25-70%, Barbera, Nebbiolo and/or Merlot 10-55%, (other local red varieties 10% max)

Torgiano UMBRIA, ITA Sangiovese 50-70%, Canaiolo 15-30%, (Trebbiano Toscano 10% max, other local red varieties 15% max). The following varietal wine is also made: Cabernet Sauvignon

Torgiano Riserva UMBRIA, ITA Sangiovese 50-70%, Canaiolo 15-30% (Trebbiano, *Ciliegiolo* and/or Montepulciano 10% max)

Toro SPAIN Tempranillo, (Garnacha)

Torres Vedras PORTUGAL Aragonez, Castelão, *Tinta Miúda,* and/or Touriga Nacional 70% min, Trincadeira 30% max, Alicante Bouschet, Cabernet Sauvignon, *Camarate, Jaén,* Syrah, Tinta Barroca an/or Touriga Franca 30% max, (*Caladoc* 15% max)

Touraine LOIRE, FRA Gamay, Cabernet Franc, (Cabernet Sauvignon, Malbec, Pinot Noir, Pinot Meunier, Pinot Gris, Pineau d'Aunis)

Touraine-Amboise LOIRE, FRA Gamay, Cabernet Franc, Cabernet Sauvignon, Malbec

Touraine-Mesland LOIRE, FRA Cabernet Franc, Cabernet Sauvignon, Malbec, Gamay

Trentino TRENTINO-ALTO ADIGE, ITA Cabernet Franc, Cabernet Sauvignon and/or Merlot 100%. The following varietal wines are also made: Cabernet Franc, Cabernet Sauvignon, Lagrein, Marzemino, Merlot, Pinot Nero, *Rebo*. Also, blended red varietal wines are made from Cabernet Franc, Cabernet Sauvignon, Merlot and Lagrein, with the first variety in the name 51-75%, and the second variety 25-49%

Trentino Sorni TRENTINO-ALTO ADIGE, ITA Teroldego, Schiava and/or Lagrein

Trentino Superiore TRENTINO-ALTO ADIGE, ITA Cabernet Franc, Cabernet Sauvignon and/or Merlot 85-100%, (Lagrein and/or *Rebo* 15% max)

Tursan SOUTHWEST, FRA Tannat, Cabernet Franc, Cabernet Sauvignon, Fer

Utiel-Requena SPAIN Bobal, Garnacha, Tempranillo, (Cabernet Sauvignon, Merlot)

Utiel-Requena Superior SPAIN Garnacha and/or Tempranillo

Vacqueyras RHÔNE, FRA Grenache 50% min, Syrah, Mourvèdre, Cinsaut, (*Terret Noir*, Counoise, *Muscardin*, *Vacarèse*, Gamay, *Camarèse*)

Val di Cornia TUSCANY, ITA Sangiovese 50% min, Cabernet Sauvignon and/or Merlot 50% max (other local red varieties 20% max). The following varietal wines are also made: Cabernet Sauvignon, Merlot, Sangiovese

Val di Cornia Suvereto TUSCANY, ITA Cabernet Sauvignon 50% min, Merlot 50% max (other local red varieties 10% max). The following varietal wines are also made: Cabernet Sauvignon, Merlot, Sangiovese

Val Polcevera LIGURIA, ITA Dolcetto, Sangiovese and/or *Ciliegiolo* 60% min, Barbera 40% max

Valcalepio LOMBARDY, ITA Merlot 40-75%, Cabernet Sauvignon 25-60%

Valdadige VENETO & TRENTINO-ALTO ADIGE, ITA *Enantio* and/or Schiava 50-100%, Merlot, Pinot Nero, Lagrein, Teroldego, Cabernet Franc and/or Cabernet Sauvignon 50% max. The following varietal wine is also made: Schiava

Valdadige Terra dei Forti Rosso Superiore VENETO & TRENTINO-ALTO ADIGE, ITA Merlot and/or *Enantio* 70-100% w/ *Enantio* 30% min, Cabernet Franc, Cabernet Sauvignon, Lagrein and/or Teroldego 30% max. The following varietal wines are also made: Cabernet Franc, Cabernet Sauvignon, *Enantio*

Valdeorras SPAIN *Mencía*, Garnacha Tintorera, *Gran Negro, María Ardoña*

Valdepeñas SPAIN Tempranillo (Garnacha, Cabernet Sauvignon, Merlot, Pinot Noir)

Valdichiana TUSCANY, ITA Sangiovese 50%, Cabernet Sauvignon, Cabernet Franc, Merlot and/or Syrah 50% max, (other local non-aromatic red varieties 15% max). The following varietal wine is also made: Sangiovese

Valençay LOIRE, FRA Cabernet Franc, Cabernet Sauvignon, Malbec, Gamay, (Pineau d'Aunis, *Gamay Teinturier*)

Valencia SPAIN Garnacha, Monsatrell, Tempranillo, Garnacha Tintorera, *Forcayat*

Valle d'Aosta AOSTA, ITA One or more local red varieties. The following varietal wines are also made: *Cornalin, Fumin,* Gamay, *Mayolet,* Merlot, Nebbiolo, *Petit Rouge, Premetta,* Syrah

Valle d'Aosta Arnad-Montjovet AOSTA, ITA Nebbiolo 70-100%, other local red varieties 30% max

Valle d'Aosta Chambave AOSTA, ITA Petit Rouge 70-100%, other local red varieties 30% max

Valle d'Aosta Donnas AOSTA, ITA Nebbiolo 85-100%, (other local red varieties 15% max)

Valle d'Aosta Enfer d'Arvier AOSTA, ITA Petit Rouge 85-100%, (other local red varieties 15% max)

Valle d'Aosta Nus AOSTA, ITA *Vien de Nus* and *Petit Rouge* 70-100%, of which *Vien de Nus* 40% min, other local red varieties 30% max

Valle d'Aosta Torrette AOSTA, ITA *Petit Rouge* 70-100%, other local red varieties 30% max

Valle de Güimár SPAIN *Listán Negro, Negramoll, Malvasía Rosada*

Valle de la Orotava SPAIN *Listán Negro,* (*Negramoll, Malvasía Rosada, Moscatel Negro, Bastardo Negro, Tintilla, Vijariego Negra*)

Valpaços PORTUGAL *Bastardo, Cornifesto, Marufo,* Trincadeira, *Tinta Carvalha,* Aragonez, Touriga Franca, Touriga Nacional

Valpolicella VENETO, ITA Corvina 40%-70%, Rondinella 20-40%, Molinara 5-25%, (Barbera, *Negrara Trentina, Rossignola,* Sangiovese)

Valsusa PIEDMONT, ITA *Avanà,* Barbera, Dolcetto and/or *Beretta Cuneese* 60%, other local non-aromatic red varieties 40% max

Valtellina LOMBARDY, ITA Nebbiolo 80%, (other local red varieties 20% max)

Velletri LATIUM, ITA Sangiovese 10-45%, Montepulciano 30-50%, (*Cesanese, Bombino Nero,* Merlot, *Ciliegiolo,* and/or other local red varieties 30% max)

Verbicaro CALABRIA, ITA Gaglioppo and/or *Greco Nero,* 60-80%, Malvasia, *Guarnaccia Bianca* and/or Greco 20-40%, (other local non-aromatic red varieties 20% max)

Verduno (Pelavrega) PIEDMONT, ITA Pelaverga Piccolo 85%, (other local non-aromatic red varieties 15% max)

Vesuvio CAMPANIA, ITA Piedirosso and/or *Sciascinoso* 80%, (Aglianico 20% max)

Vicenza VENETO, ITA Merlot 50%, other local non-aromatic red varieties 50% max. The following varietal wines are also made: Cabernet Sauvignon, Merlot, Pinot Nero, *Raboso*

Vignanello LATIUM, ITA Sangiovese 40-60%, *Ciliegiolo* 40-50% (other local red varieties 20% max)

Vin du Bugey SAVOIE, FRA Gamay, Pinot Noir, *Poulsard, Mondeuse,* Pinot Noir (Chardonnay, *Roussette,* Aligoté, *Mondeuse Blanc, Jacquère,* Pinot Gris)

Vin de Corse CORSICA, FRA *Nielluccio ,* Grenache, *Sciacarello,* (Cinsaut, Mourvedré, *Barbarossa,* Syrah, Carginan, Vermentino)

Vin du Savoie SAVOIE, FRA Gamay, *Mondeuse,* Pinot Noir, (*Persan,* Cabernet Franc, Cabernet Sauvignon, *Etraire de la Dui, Serène, Joubertin,* Chardonnay, *Roussette,* Aligoté, *Mondeuse Blanc, Jacquère,* Pinot Gris, *Gringet, Verdesse,* Chasselas)

Vinho Verde PORTUGAL *Amaral, Borraçal, Alvarelhão, Espadeiro, Padeiro, Pedral, Rabo de Anho, Vinhão*

Vino Nobile di Montepulciano TUSCANY, ITA Sangiovese 70% min, (Canaiolo 20% max, other local red varieties 20% max, local white varieties 10% max)

Vinos de Madrid SPAIN Tempranillo, Garnacha

Vins d'Entraygues et du Fel SOUTHWEST, FRA Cabernet Franc, Cabernet Sauvignon, Fer, Gamay, *Jurançon Noir,* Merlot, *Mouyssaguès,* Négrette, Pinot Noir

Vins d'Estaing SOUTHWEST, FRA Fer, Gamay, *Abouriou, Jurançon Noir,* Merlot, *Mouyssaguès,* Négrette, Pinot Noir, *Duras, Castet*

Vins de Lavilledieu SOUTHWEST, FRA Mauzac, *Merille,* Cinsault, *Fuella,* Négrette 80% min, (Syrah, Gamay, *Jurançon Noir, Picpoul Noir, Milgranet,* Fer 20% max)

Vins de l'Orléanais LOIRE, FRA Pinot Noir, Pinot Meunier, Cabernet Franc

Vins du Thouarsais LOIRE, FRA Cabernet Franc, Cabernet Sauvignon, Gamay

Volnay BURGUNDY, FRA Pinot Noir, (Pinot Gris and Pinot Liébault allowed but virtually never used)

Volnay-Santenots BURGUNDY, FRA Pinot Noir, (Pinot Gris and Pinot Liébault allowed but virtually never used)

Vosne-Romanée BURGUNDY, FRA Pinot Noir, (Pinot Gris and Pinot Liébault allowed but virtually never used)

Vougeot BURGUNDY, FRA Pinot Noir, (Pinot Gris and Pinot Liébault allowed but virtually never used)

Ycoden-Daute-Isora SPAIN *Bastardo Negra, Listán Negro, Malvasía Rosada, Moscatel Negro, Negramoll, Tintilla, Vijariego Negra*

Yecla SPAIN Monastrell, Garnacha, (Tempranillo, Cabernet Sauvignon, Merlot, Syrah)

WHITE WINES INDEX

Ajaccio CORSICA, FRA Ugni Blanc, Vermentino

Abona SPAIN Palomino, (*Bermejuela, Bastardo Blanco, Gual,* Malvasía, Moscatel, Pedro Ximénez, *Sabro,* Torrontés, Verdello, *Vijariego*)

Alcobaço PORTUGAL Arinto, *Fernão Pires,* Malvasia, Tamarez and/or *Vital* 80% min w/ *Fernão Pires* and/or *Vital* at 50% min (other local varieties 20% max)

Alella SPAIN Xarel-lo, Garnacha Blanca, (*Pansá Rosada,* Picpoul Blanc, Malvasía, Parellada, Macabeo, Chardonnay Chenin Blanc)

Alicante SPAIN *Merseguera, Moscatel Romano,* Macabeo, Airén (*Planta Fin,* Riesling, Chardonnay)

Almansa SPAIN Airén, *Merseguera*

Anhialos GREECE Rhoditis, (Savatiano)

Anjou LOIRE, FRA Chenin Blanc 80% min, (Chardonnay, Sauvignon Blanc)

Albana di Romagna EMILIA-ROMAGNA, ITA Albana

Alghero SARDINIA, ITA One or more local non-aromatic white varieties

Alenquer PORTUGAL Arinto, *Fernão Pires, Rabo de Ovelha, Seara Nova* and/or *Vital* 65% min, *Alicante Branco,* Alvarinho, Chardonnay, *Jampal,* Malvasia Rei, *Ratinho,* Sauvignon Blanc and/or *Viosinho* 35% max

Alentejo Borba PORTUGAL *Antão Vaz,* Arinto, *Perrum,* Rabo de Ovelha, *Síria* and/or Trincadeira 95% min, *Alicante Branco* 5% max

Alentejo Évora PORTUGAL *Antão Vaz,* Arinto, *Perrum* and/or Síria 75% min, Diagalves, *Fernão Pires,* Malvasia Rei, *Manteúdo,* Rabo de Ovelha and/or Trincadeira

Alentejo Granja/Amareleja PORTUGAL *Antão Vaz, Perrum,* Rabo de Ovelha and/or *Síria* 65%, *Diagalves, Manteúdo,* and/or Trincadeira 35% max

Alentejo Moura PORTUGAL *Antão Vaz,* Arinto, *Fernão Pires, Rabo de Ovelha* and/or *Síria* 70% min, *Alicante Branco,* Bical, Chardonnay, *Moscatel Graúdo, Perrum* and/or Trincadeira 30% max

Alentejo Portalegre PORTUGAL Arinto, *Fernão Pires, Malvasia Rei, Síria* and/or Trincadeira 75% min, *Alicante Branco, Diagalves* and/or *Manteúdo* 25% max

Alentejo Redondo PORTUGAL *Antão Vaz,* Arinto, *Fernão Pires, Rabo de Ovelha, Síria* and/or Trincadeira 75% min, *Diagalves* and/or *Manteúdo* 25% max

Alentejo Reguengos PORTUGAL *Antão Vaz,* Arinto, *Perrum, Rabo de Ovelha, Síria* and/or Trincadeira 75% min, *Diagalves, Fernão Pires* and/or *Manteúdo* 25%

Alentejo Vidigueira PORTUGAL *Antão Vaz,* Arinto, *Fernão Pires, Perrum, Rabo de Ovelha* and/or *Síria* 75% min, *Alicante Branco, Diagalves, Larião, Manteúdo, Mourisco Branco* and/or Trincadeira 25% max

Aloxe Corton BURGUNDY, FRA Chardonnay

Ampurdán-Costa Brava SPAIN Macabeo, Garnacha Blanca, Chardonnay, (Chenin Blanc, Riesling, Xarel-lo, Gewürztraminer, Parellada)

Anhialos GREECE Roditis 50%, Savatiano 50%

Ansonica Costa dell'Argentario TUSCANY, ITA Ansonica 85% (other local varieties, 15% max)

Arbois JURA, FRA Savagnin, Chardonnay, Pinot Blanc

Arbois Pupillin JURA, FRA Savagnin, Chardonnay, Pinot Blanc

Arbois Vin Jaune JURA, FRA Savagnin

Arborea SARDINIA, ITA Trebbiano

Arcole VENETO, ITA Garganega 50% min, other local non-aromatic white varieties 50% max

Arneis di Roero PIEDMONT, ITA Arneis

Arruda PORTUGAL Arinto, *Fernão Pires*, Rabo de Ovelha, *Seara Nova* and/or *Vital* 70% min, *Alicante Branco*, Chardonnay, *Jampal*, Malvasia Rei, Sauvignon Blanc and/or *Viosinho* 30% max

Assisi UMBRIA, ITA Trebbiano 50-70%, Grechetto 10-30%, other local white varieties 40% max

Auxey-Duresses BURGUNDY, FRA Chardonnay, (Pinot Blanc)

Aversa CAMPANIA, ITA *Asprinio* 85% min, other local white varieties 15% max

Bagnoli (di Sopra) VENETO, ITA Chardonnay 30-70%, Sauvignon Blanc and/or Tocai Friulano 20-60%, *Raboso Piave* and/or *Raboso Veronese* 10-50%, (other local white varieities 10% max)

Bairrada PORTUGAL Arinto, Bical, *Cercial*, Chardonnay, *Fernão Pires*, Rabo de Ovelha, Sauvignon Blanc, *Sercialinho*, Verdelho

Bandol PROVENCE, FRA Bourboulenc, Clairette, Trebbiano, Sauvignon Blanc

Bâtard-Montrachet BURGUNDY, FRA Chardonnay

Béarn SOUTHWEST, FRA Petit Manseng, Gros Manseng, (*Corbu, Lauzet, Camaralet, Raffiat,* Sauvignon Blanc)

Beaujolais BURGUNDY, FRA Chardonnay, Aligoté

Beaujolais Supérieur BURGUNDY, FRA Chardonnay, Aligoté

Beaujolais Villages BURGUNDY, FRA Chardonnay, Aligoté

Beaune BURGUNDY, FRA Chardonnay, (Pinot Blanc)

Beira Interior Castelo Rodrigo PORTUGAL Malvasia Fina, *Síria* and/or *Tamarez* 80% min (Bical, Arinto, Malvasia Rei, *Rabo de Ovelha* and/or *Vital* 20% max)

Beira Interior Cova da Beira PORTUGAL *Alicante Branco*, Arinto, Bical, *Fonte Cal*, Malvasia Fina, Malvasia Rei, Rabo de Ovelha and/or *Síria* 80% min, (Tamarez 20% max)

Beira Interior Pinhel PORTUGAL Bical, Arinto (Pedernã), *Fonte Cal*, Malvasia Fina, Malvasia Rei, *Rabo de Ovelha*, *Síria*, and/or *Tamarez* 80% min (other local varieties 20% max)

Bellet PROVENCE, FRA *Rolle*, Ugni Blanc, *Mayorquin*, (Clairette, Bourboulenc, Chardonnay, *Pignerol,* Muscat Blanc)

Bergerac SOUTHWEST, FRA Sémillon, Sauvignon Blanc, Muscadelle, *Ondenc*, Chenin Blanc, (Ugni Blanc)

Bergerac Sec SOUTHWEST, FRA Sémillon, Sauvignon Blanc, Muscadelle, *Ondenc*, Chenin Blanc, (Ugni Blanc)

Bianchello del Metauro MARCHES, ITA *Bianchello/Biancame*, (with the possible addition of Malvasia Toscana 5% max)

Bianco Capena LATIUM, ITA Malvasia di Candia 55% min, Trebbiano Toscano, *Romagnolo*, *Giallo* 25% min, (*Bellone* and Bombino 20% max)

Bianco d'Alcamo SICILY, ITA Catarratto 80% min, (*Grecanico*, Inzolia, *Grillo*, Chardonnay, Müller Thurgau and/or Sauvignon Blanc 20% max)

Bianco della Valdinievole TUSCANY, ITA Trebbiano Toscano 70% min (Malvasia del Chianti, *Canaiolo Bianco* and/or Vermentino 25% max, other local white varieties 5% max)

Bianco dell'Empolese TUSCANY, ITA Trebbiano Toscano 80%, (other local white varieties 20% max)

Bianco di Custoza VENETO, ITA Trebbiano Toscano 20-45%, Garganega 20-40%, Tocai Friulano 5-30%, Cortese, Riesling Italico, Pinot Bianco, Chardonnay and/or Malvasia Toscana 20-30%

Bianco di Pitigliano TUSCANY, ITA Trebbiano Toscano 50-80% (Greco, Malvasia Bianca Toscana and/or Verdello 20%, Grechetto 15% max, Chardonnay, Sauvignon Blanc, Pinot Bianco and/or Riesling Italico 15% max, other local white varieties 10% max)

Bianco Pisano di San Torpé TUSCANY, ITA Trebbiano Toscano 75%, other local white varieties 25% max

Bienvenues-Bâtard-Montrachet BURGUNDY, FRA Chardonnay

Bierzo SPAIN *Doña Blanca*, Godello, Malvasía, Palomino

Biferno MOLISES, ITA Trebbiano Toscano 65-70%, Bombino Bianco 25-30% (Malvasia Bianca 5-10%)

Binissalem SPAIN *Moll* 70% min, (Macabeo, Parellada)

Bivongi CALABRIA, ITA Greco, *Guardavalle* and/or *Montonico* 30-50%, Malvasia and/or Ansonica 30-50%, other local white varieties 30% max

Bizkaiako Txacoli SPAIN Hondarrabi Zuri

Blaye BORDEAUX, FRA Ugni Blanc, (Folle Blanche, Colombard, Chenin Blanc, Sémillon, Sauvingon Blanc, Muscadelle 10% max)

Bolgheri TUSCANY, ITA Trebbiano Toscano, Vermentino and/or Sauvignon Blanc 10-70%, other local white varieties 30% max. The following varietal wines are also made: Sauvignon Blanc, Vermentino

Bordeaux BORDEAUX, FRA Sémillon, Sauvignon Blanc, Muscadelle 70% min, *Merlot Blanc*, Colombard, Mauzac, *Ondenc*, Ugni Blanc 30% max

Bordeaux-Côtes-de-Francs BORDEAUX, FRA Sémillon, Sauvignon Blanc, (Muscadelle)

Bordeaux Haut-Benauge BORDEAUX, FRA Sémillon, Sauvignon Blanc, (Muscadelle)

Bordeaux Sec BORDEAUX, FRA Sémillon, Sauvignon Blanc, Muscadelle 70% min, *Merlot Blanc*, Colombard, Mauzac, Ondenc, Ugni Blanc 30% max

Bosco Eliceo EMILIA-ROMAGNA, ITA Trebbiano 70% min, Malvasia and/or Sauvignon Blanc 30% max

Bourg BORDEAUX, FRA Sauvingon Blanc, Sémillon, Muscadelle, Colombard, *Merlot Blanc*, (Chenin Blanc 10% max)

Bourgogne BURGUNDY, FRA Chardonnay, (Pinot Blanc)

Bourgogne Aligoté BURGUNDY, FRA Aligoté, (Chardonnay)

Bourgogne Côtes d'Auxerre BURGUNDY, FRA Chardonnay

Bourgogne Côte St.-Jacques BURGUNDY, FRA Chardonnay

Bourgogne Grand Ordinaire BURGUNDY, FRA Chardonnay, Aligoté, Pinot Blanc, Melon de Bourgogne, (*Sacy*)

Breganze VENETO, ITA Tocai Friulano 85% (other local non-aromatic white varieties 15% max)

Bucelas PORTUGAL Arinto 75% min, Sercial and/or *Rabo de Ovelha* 25% max

Bullas SPAIN Macabeo, Airén

Buzet SOUTHWEST, FRA Sémillon, Sauvignon Blanc, Muscadelle

Cagnina di Romagna EMILIA-ROMAGNA, ITA Refosco 85% min, (other local red varieties 15% max)

Calatayud SPAIN Macabeo, Malvasía, (Moscatel Blanco & Garnacha Blanca)

Caluso PIEDMONT, ITA Erbaluce

Campi Flegrei CAMPANIA, ITA Falanghina 50-70%, *Biancolella* and/or Coda di Volpe 10-30%, other local white varieties 30% max

Campo de Borja SPAIN Macabeo

Canavese PIEDMONT, ITA Erbaluce

Candia dei Colli Apuani TUSCANY, ITA Vermentino 70-80%, (*Albarola* 10-20%, *Trebbiano* and/or Malvasia del Chianti 20%)

Capri CAMPANIA, ITA Falanghina and Greco, of which Greco 50% max, (Biancolella 20%)

Cassis PROVENCE, FRA Ugni Blanc, Sauvignon Blanc, Bourboulenc, Clairette, Marsanne, *Pascal Blanc*

Castel del Monte APULIA, ITA *Pampanuto*, Chardonnay, Bombino Bianco

Castel San Lorenzo CAMPANIA, ITA Trebbiano 50-60%, Malvasia 30-40%, (other local white varieties 20% max)

Castelli Romani LATIUM, ITA Malvasia Bianca, Malvasia di Candia, Malvasia Puntinata, and/or Trebbiano 70% (other local white varieties 30% max)

Cariñena SPAIN Macabeo, (Garnacha Blanca, Parellada, Moscatel Romano, Chardonnay)

Cerveteri LATIUM, ITA Trebbiano Toscano, Trebbiano Romagnolo and Trebbiano Giallo 50% min, Malvasia di Candia and Malvasia del Lazo 35% max, (Tocai Friulano, Verdicchio, *Bellone* and/or Bombino Bianco, 15% max)

Chablis BURGUNDY, FRA Chardonnay

Chablis Grand Cru BURGUNDY, FRA Chardonnay

Chablis Premier Cru BURGUNDY, FRA Chardonnay

Chacolí de Guetaria SPAIN Hondarrabi Zuri

Chacolí de Vizcaya SPAIN Hondarrabi Zuri

Charlemagne BURGUNDY, FRA Chardonnay, Aligoté

Chassagne-Montrachet BURGUNDY, FRA Chardonnay, (Pinot Blanc)

Château-Chalon JURA, FRA Savagnin

Château Grillet RHÔNE, FRA Viognier

Châteauneuf-du-Pape RHÔNE, FRA Grenache Blanc, Bourboulenc, Roussanne, (Clairette, Picpoul Blanc)

Châtillon-en-Diois RHÔNE, FRA Chardonnay, Aligoté

Chaves PORTUGAL *Roupeiro*, Gouveio and/or Malvasia Fina 70% min (other local varieties 30% max)

Chevalier-Montrachet BURGUNDY, FRA Chardonnay

Cheverny LOIRE, FRA Sauvignon Blanc 65-80%, (Chardonnay, Chenin Blanc, *Arbois*)

Chinon LOIRE, FRA Chenin Blanc

Cilento CAMPANIA, ITA Fiano 60-65%, Trebbiano 20-30%, (Greco and/or Malvasia 10-15%, other local white varieties 10% max)

Cinque Terre LIGURIA, ITA *Bosco* 40% min, (*Albarola* and/or Vermentino 20% max, other local varieties 20% max)

Circeo LATIUM, ITA Trebbiano Toscano 60% min, Malvasia di Candia 30% max, other local white varieties 30% max

Cirò CALABRIA, ITA Greco 90% min, (Trebbiano)

Clairette de Bellegarde LANGUEDOC-ROUSSILLON, FRA Clairette

Clairette du Languedoc LANGUEDOC-ROUSSILLON, FRA Clairette

Colares PORTUGAL Malvasia - grown in sand - 80% min (other local varieties 20% max)

Colli Albani LATIUM, ITA Malvasia di Candia 60% max, Trebbiano Toscano, Trebbiano Romagnolo, Trebbiano Giallo and/or Trebbiano di Soave 25-50%, Malvasia del Lazio 5-45%, (other local white varieties 10% max)

Colli Altotiberini UMBRIA, ITA Trebbiano toscano 75-90%, (Malvasia del Chianti 10%, other local white varieties 15% max)

Colli Amerini UMBRIA, ITA Trebbiano toscano 70-85%, Grechetto, Verdello, Garganega and/or Malvasia Toscana 30% max, (other local white varieties 15% max)

Colli Berici VENETO, ITA The following varietal wines are also made: Chardonnay, Garganega, Pinot Bianco, Sauvignon Blanc, *Tocai Italico*

Colli Bolognese EMILIA-ROMAGNA, ITA *Albana* 60-80%, Trebbiano 20-40%

Colli Bolognese Classico Pignoletto EMILIA-ROMAGNA, ITA *Pignoletto* 85% min, (Pinot Bianco, Riesling Italico and or Trebbiano Romagnolo 15% max)

Colli del Trasimeno UMBRIA, ITA Trebbiano 40%, Grechetto, Chardonnay, Pinot Blanc and/or Pinot Grigio 30%, other local white varieties 30% max

Colli della Romagna Centrale EMILIA-ROMAGNA, ITA Chardonnay 50-60%, Bombino, Sauvignon Blanc, Trebbiano and/or Pinot Bianco 40-50%

Colli della Sabina LATIUM, ITA Trebbiano Toscano and/or Trebbiano Giallo 40%, Malvasia del Lazio and/or Malvasia di Candia 40%, (other local white varieties 20% max)

Colli dell'Etruria Centrale TUSCANY, ITA Trebbiano Toscano 50%, Malvasia del Chianti, Pinot Bianco, Pinot Grigio, Chardonnay, Sauvignon Blanc and/or Vernaccia 50% max, other local white varieties 25% max

Colli di Conegliano VENETO, ITA *Incrocio Manzoni 6.0.13* 30% max, Pinot Bianco and/or Chardonnay 30%, (Sauvignon Blanc and or Riesling Renano 10% max)

Colli di Faenza EMILIA-ROMAGNA, ITA Chardonnay 40-60%, Trebbiano, Sauvignon Blanc, Pinot Bianco, and/or *Pignoletto* 40-60%

Colli di Luni LIGURIA / TUSCANY, ITA Vermentino 35%, Trebbiano Toscano 25-40%, other local white varieties 30% max

Colli di Parma EMILIA-ROMAGNA, ITA The following varietal wines are also made: Chardonnay, Malvasia, Pinot Bianco, Pinot Grigio, Sauvignon Blanc

Colli di Rimini EMILIA-ROMAGNA, ITA Trebbiano Romagnolo 50-70%, *Biancame* and/or *Mostosa* 30-50%, (other local white varieties 20% max)

Colli di Scandiano e Canossa EMILIA-ROMAGNA, ITA Sauvignon Blanc 40-80%, Malvasia, Trebbiano, Pinot Bianco and/or Pinot Grigi 20-60%

Colli d'Imola EMILIA-ROMAGNA, ITA Chardonnay, *Pignoletto,* Trebbiano

Colli Etruschi Viterbesi LATIUM, ITA Trebbiano Toscano 40-80%, Malvasia Toscana and/or Malvasia del Lazio 30% max, other local white varieties 30% max. The following varietal wines are also made: Grechetto, Moscatello, *Procanico*, *Rossetto*

Colli Euganei VENETO, ITA Garganega 30-50%, Prosecco 10-30%, Tocai Friulano and/or Sauvignon Blanc 20-40%, (Chardonnay, Pinot Bianco, Riesling Italico and/or *Pinella* 20% max). The following varietal wines are also made: Chardonnay, *Fior d'Arancio*, Pinot Bianco, *Tocai Italico*, *Pinello, Serpino*

Colli Lanuvini LATIUM, ITA Malvasia di Candia and/or Malvasia Puntinata 70% max, Trebbiano 30% (other local white varieties 10% max)

Colli Maceratesi MARCHES, ITA Maceratino 70%, Trebbiano Toscano, Verdicchio, Malvasia Toscana, Chardonnay, Sauvignon Blanc, Incrocio Bruni 54, Pecorino and/or Grechetto 30% max (other local white varieties 15% max)

Colli Martani UMBRIA, ITA Grechetto or Trebbiano Toscano 85% (Grechetto, Trebbiano, Malvasia, Garganega and/or Verdicchio 15% max)

Colli Orientali del Friuli FRIULI-VENEZIA GIULIA, ITA One or more local white varieties as a blend. The following varietal wines are also made: Chardonnay, Malvasia, *Picolit*, Pinot Bianco, Pinot Grigio, *Ribolla Gialla*, Riseling, Sauvignon Blanc, Tocai Friulano, *Traminer Aromatico, Verduzzo Friulano*

Colli Perugini Umbria, ITA Trebbiano Toscano 50% min, other local white varieties 50% max (Malvasia 10% max)

Colli Pesaresi Marches, ITA Trebbiano Toscano, Verdicchio, *Biancame*, Pinot Grigio, Pinot Nero, Riesling Italico, Chardonnay, Sauvignon Blanc and/or Pinot Bianco 75% min, other local non-aromatic white varieties 25% max. The following varietal wines are also made: *Biancame*, Trebbiano

Colli Pesaresi Roncaglia Bianco Marches, ITA Trebbiano Toscano 85% (Pinot Nero 15%)

Colli Piacentini EMILIA-ROMAGNA, ITA The following varietal wines are also made: Chardonnay, Malvasia, *Ortrugo*, Pinot Grigio, Sauvignon Blanc

Colli Piacentini Monterosso Val D'Arda EMILIA-ROMAGNA, ITA Malvasia and/or Moscato Bianco 20-50%, Trebbiano and/or *Ortrugo* 20-50%, *Bervedino*, Sauvignon Blanc and/or other local white varieties 30% max

Colli Piacentini Trebbianino Val Trebbia EMILIA-ROMAGNA, ITA *Ortrugo* 35-65%, Trebbiano and/or Sauvignon Blanc 15-30%, (Malvasia and/or Moscato Bianco 10-20%, other local white varieties 15% max)

Colli Piacentini Valnure EMILIA-ROMAGNA, ITA Malvasia 20-50%, *Ortrugo* and/or Trebbiano 20-65%, (other local white varieties 15% max)

Colli Tortonesi PIEDMONT, ITA One or more local non-aromatic white varieties as a blend. The following varietal wine is also made: Cortese

Colline di Levanto LIGURIA, ITA Vermentino 40%, other local white varieties 35% max, (*Albarola* 20%, *Bosco* 5%)

Colline Lucchesi TUSCANY, ITA Trebbiano 45-70%, Greco, Grechetto, Vermentino and/or Malvasia del Chianti 45% max, Chardonnay and/or Sauvignon 30% max, (other local white varieties 15% max). The following varietal wines are also made: Sauvignon Blanc, Vermentino

Colline Novaresi PIEDMONT, ITA Erbaluce

Collio Goriziano FRIULI-VENEZIA GIULIA, ITA One or more local white varieties as a blend with (Müller Thurgau and/or Gewürtzraminer 20% max). The following varietal wines are also made: Chardonnay, Müller Thurgau, Malvasia, Pinot Bianco, Pinot Grigio, *Ribolla Gialla*, Riesling, Riesling Italico, Sauvignon Blanc,Tocai Friulano, Traminer Aromatico

Conca de Barberá SPAIN Macabeo, Parellada (Chardonnay)

Condado de Huelva SPAIN *Zalema*, (Palomino, *Garrido Fino*, Moscatel)

Condrieu RHÔNE, FRA Viognier

Contea di Sclafani SICILY, ITA Catarratto, Inzolia and/or *Grecanico* 50%; other local white varieties 50% max. The following varietal wines are also made: Catarratto, Chardonnay, *Grecanico*, *Grillo*, Inzolia, Pinot Bianco, Sauvignon Blanc

Contessa Entellina SICILY, ITA Inzolia 50%, Catarratto, *Grecanico*, Chardonnay, Sauvignon Blanc, Müller Thurgau, Pinot Bianco and/or *Grillo* 35%, (other local varieties 15% max). The following varietal wines are also made: Chardonnay, *Grecanico*, Inzolia, Sauvignon Blanc

Controguerra ABRUZZO, ITA Trebbiano 60% min, other local white varieties 25% max, (*Passerina* 15% min)

Corbières LANGUEDOC-ROUSSILLON, FRA Bourboulenc, Grenache Blanc, Macabeo, (Clairette, Muscat, Picpoul Blanc, *Terret Gris*, Marsanne, Roussanne, Vermentino)

Cori LATIUM, ITA Malvasia di Candia 70% max, Trebbiano Toscano 40% max, *Bellone* and/or Trebbiano Giallo 30% max

Cortese dell'Alto Monferrato PIEDMONT, ITA Cortese 85% (other local white varieties 15% max)

Cortese di Gavi PIEDMONT, ITA Cortese

Corton BURGUNDY, FRA Chardonnay

Corton-Charlemagne BURGUNDY, FRA Chardonnay

Cortona TUSCANY, ITA The following varietal wines are also made: Chardonnay, Grechetto, Pinot Bianco, Riesling Italico, Sauvignon Blanc

Costa d'Amalfi CAMPANIA, ITA Falanghina and/or *Biancolella* 60%, other local white varieties 40% max

Coste della Sesia PIEDMONT, ITA Erbaluce

Costers del Segre SPAIN Macabeo, Parellada, Xarel-lo, Chardonnay, Garnacha Blanca (Sauvignon Blanc, Albariño)

Costières de Nîmes LANGUEDOC-ROUSSILLON, FRA Clairette, Bourboulenc, Grenache Blanc, Ugni Blanc, Roussanne, Marsanne, Macabéo, *Rolle*

Coteaux d'Aix-en-Provence PROVENCE, FRA Bourboulenc, Clairette, Grenache Blanc, Vermentino, Ugni Blanc, Sauvignon Blanc, Sémillon

Coteaux d'Ancenis LOIRE, FRA Chenin Blanc, Pinot Gris

Coteaux de Die RHÔNE, FRA Clairette

Coteaux du Giennois BURGUNDY, FRA Sauvignon Blanc

Coteaux du Giennois Cosne-sur-Loire BURGUNDY, FRA Sauvignon Blanc

Coteaux du Languedoc LANGUEDOC-ROUSSILLON, FRA Bourboulenc, Grenache Blanc, Clairette, Picpoul Blanc, (Ugni Blanc, Roussanne, Marsanne, Macabéo, *Rolle, Terret Blanc, Carignan Blanc*)

Coteaux de Loir LOIRE, FRA Chenin Blanc

Coteaux du Lyonnais BURGUNDY, FRA Chardonnay, Aligoté

Coteaux de Pierrevert RHÔNE, FRA Clairette, Picpoul Blanc, Marsanne, Roussanne, Ugni Blanc

Coteaux de Tricastin RHÔNE, FRA Grenache Blanc, Clairette, Bourbolenc, Picpoul Blanc, (Ugni Blanc, Roussanne, Marsanne, Viognier)

Coteaux de Vendômois LOIRE, FRA Chenin Blanc 80% min, (Chardonnay)

Coteaux Varois PROVENCE, FRA Vermentino, Clairette, Grenache Blanc, Ugni Blanc, Sémillon

Côtes d'Auvergne LOIRE, FRA Chardonnay

Côtes de Blaye BORDEAUX, FRA Sauvingon Blanc, Sémillon, Muscadelle, (Colombard, *Merlot Blanc,* Folle Blanche, Chenin Blanc)

Côte de Beaune BURGUNDY, FRA Chardonnay, (Pinot Blanc)

Côtes de Duras SOUTHWEST, FRA Sauvingon Blanc, Sémillon, Muscadelle, *Mauzac,* Chenin Blanc, *Ondenc,* (Ugni Blanc)

Côtes du Jura JURA, FRA Savagnin, Chardonnay

Côtes du Jura Vin Jaune JURA, FRA Savagnin

Côtes du Lubéron RHÔNE, FRA Grenache Blanc, Clairette, Bourbolenc, Vermentino, Ugni Blanc, Roussanne, Marsanne

Côtes du Marmandais SOUTHWEST, FRA Sauvingon Blanc 70% min, (Ugni Blanc, Sémillon)

Côtes de Meliton GREECE *Athiri* 50%, Rodítis 35% (Assyrtiko 15%)

Côtes de Millau LANGUEDOC-ROUSSILLON, FRA Chenin Blanc, Mauzac

Côtes de Provence PROVENCE, FRA Clairette, Vermentino, Ugni Blanc, Sémillon

Côtes-du-Rhône RHÔNE, FRA Clairette, Roussanne, Bourboulenc, (Viognier, Picpoul Blanc, Marsanne, Grenache Blanc, *Picardan*, Mauzac, *Pascal Blanc*)

Côtes-du-Rhône-Villages RHÔNE, FRA Clairette, Roussanne, Bourboulenc, (Viognier, Picpoul Blanc, Marsanne, Grenache Blanc, *Picardan*, Mauzac, *Pascal Blanc*)

Côtes du Roussillon LANGUEDOC-ROUSSILLON, FRA Grenache Blanc, Macabéo, *Tourbat Blanc,* Marsanne, Roussanne, Vermentino

Côtes de St.-Mont SOUTHWEST, FRA *Arrufiac,* Clairette, *Courbu,* (Petit Manseng, Gros Manseng)

Côtes de Toul LORRAINE, FRA Aligoté, Auxerrois, *Aubin*

Côtes du Ventoux RHÔNE, FRA Clairette, Bourboulenc, (Grenache Blanc, Roussanne)

Côtes du Vivarais RHÔNE, FRA Clairette, Grenache Blanc, Marsanne

Crépy SAVOIE, FRA Chasselas

Criots-Bâtard-Montrachet BURGUNDY, FRA Chardonnay

Crozes-Hermitage RHÔNE, FRA Roussanne, Marsanne

Dão PORTUGAL *Barcelo,* Bical, *Cercial, Encruzado,* Malvasia Fina, *Rabo de Ovelha, Terrantez, Uva Cão,* Verdelho

Dão Nobre PORTUGAL *Encruzado* 15% min, Bical, *Cercial,* Malvasia Fina and/or Verdelho 85% max

Delia Nivolelli SICILY, ITA *Grecanico,* Inzolia and/or *Grillo,* 65%, other local white varieties 35% max. The following varietal wines are also made: Chardonnay, *Damaschino, Grecanico, Grillo,* Inzolia, Müller Thurgau, Sauvignon Blanc

Dolcetto delle Langhe Monregalesi PIEDMONT, ITA Dolcetto

Donnici CALABRIA, ITA *Montonico Bianco* 50%, Greco, Malvasia and/or *Pecorello Bianco* 30% max, (other local white varieties up to 20%)

Douro PORTUGAL *Alicante Branco, Alvarelhão Branco,* Arinto, Avesso, *Batoca,* Bical, *Branco Especial, Branco Guimarães, Caramela, Carrega Branco, Cercial,* Chasselas, *Côdega de Larinho, Diagalves, Dona Branca, Donzelinho Branco, Estreito Macio, Fernão Pires, Folgasão, Gouveio, Gouveio Estimado, Gouveio Real, Jampal,* Malvasia Fina, Malvasia Parda, Malvasia Rei, Moscadet, *Moscatel Galego Branco, Mourisco Branco, Pé Comprido, Pinheira Branca, Praça, Rabigato, Rabigato Franco, Rabigato Moreno, Rabo de Ovelha, Ratinho, Samarrinho, Sarigo,* Semillon, Sercial, *Roupeiro, Tália, Tamarez, Terrantez, Touriga Branca, Trigueira, Valente, Verdial Branco, Viosinho, Vital*

El Hierro SPAIN Palomino, *Vermejuela, Vijariego.* The following varietal wines are also made: Pedro Ximénez, Verdello, *Breval, Diego, Gual,* Malvasía, Moscatel

Elba TUSCANY, ITA Trebbiano Toscano 80-100% (other local white varieties 20% max). The following varietal wine is also made: *Ansonica*

Encostas De Aire PORTUGAL Arinto, *Fernão Pires,* Malvasia, *Tamarez* and/or *Vital* 50% min, other local varieties 50% max

Entre-Deux-Mers BORDEAUX, FRA Sémillon, Sauvignon Blanc, Muscadelle, (Colombard, Ugni Blanc, Mauzac, *Merlot Blanc*)

Entre-Deux-Mers Haut-Benauge BORDEAUX, FRA Sémillon, Sauvignon Blanc, Muscadelle, (Colombard, Ugni Blanc, Mauzac, *Merlot Blanc*)

Esino MARCHES, ITA Verdicchio 50%, other local white varieties 50% max

Est! Est!! Est!!! di Montefiascone LATIUM, ITA Trebbiano Toscano 65%, (Malvasia Toscana 20% max, Trebbiano Giallo 15% max)

Etna SICILY, ITA *Carricante* 60%, Catarratto 40% max, (Trebbiano, *Minnella Bianca* and/or other local non-aromatic white varieties 15% max)

Etna Superiore SICILY, ITA ITA *Carricante* 60%, Catarratto 20% max

Falerio MARCHES, ITA Trebbiano Toscano 20-50%, *Passerina* 10-30%, *Pecorino* 10-30% (other local white varieties 20% max)

Falerno del Massico CAMPANIA, ITA Falanghina

Fiano di Avellino CAMPANIA, ITA Fiano 85% min, (Greco and/or Coda di Volpe Bianca and/or Trebbiano)

Fiefs Vendéens LOIRE, FRA Chenin Blanc, (Sauvignon Blanc, Chardonnay)

Fixin BURGUNDY, FRA Chardonnay, (Pinot Blanc)

Frascati LATIUM, ITA Malvasia di Candia and/or Trebbiano Toscano 70% min, Greco and/or Malvasia del Lazio 30% max, (other local white varieties 10% max)

Friuli Annia FRIULI-VENEZIA GIULIA, ITA One or more local white varieties as a blend. The following varietal wines are also made: Chardonnay, Malvasia, Pinot Bianco, Pinot Grigio, Sauvignon Blanc, Tocai Friulano, *Verduzzo Friulano*

Friuli Aquileia FRIULI-VENEZIA GIULIA, ITA One or more local white varieties as a blend. The following varietal wines are also made: Chardonnay, Müller Thurgau, Malvasia Istriana, Pinot Bianco, Pinot Grigio, Riesling, Sauvignon Blanc, Tocai Friulano, Traminer Aromatico, *Verduzzo Friulano*

Friuli Grave FRIULI-VENEZIA GIULIA, ITA One or more local white varieties as a blend. The following varietal wines are also made: Chardonnay, Pinot Bianco, Pinot Grigio, Riesling, Sauvignon Blanc, Tocai Friulano, Traminer Aromatico, *Verduzzo Friulano*

Friuli Isonzo FRIULI-VENEZIA GIULIA, ITA One or more local white varieties as a blend. The following varietal wines are also made: Chardonnay, Malvasia Istriana, Pinot Bianco, Pinot Grigio, Riesling, Riesling Italico, Sauvignon Blanc, Tocai Friulano, Traminer Aromatico, *Verduzzo Friulano*

Friuli Latisana FRIULI-VENEZIA GIULIA, ITA The following varietal wines are also made: Chardonnay, Malvasia, Pinot Bianco, Pinot Grigio, Riesling, Sauvignon Blanc, Tocai Friulano, Traminer Aromatico, *Verduzzo Friulano*

Gaillac SOUTHWEST, FRA Len de l'El, Sauvignon Blanc, Mauzac, *Mauzac Rose*, Muscadelle, *Ondenc*, Sémillion

Gaillac Premières Côtes SOUTHWEST, FRA Len de l'El, Sauvignon Blanc, Mauzac, *Mauzac Rose*, Muscadelle, *Ondenc*, Sémillion

Galantina APULIA , ITA Chardonnay 55% min, (non-aromatic local white varieties)

Gallucio CAMPANIA, ITA Falanghina 70% min, (other local white varieties up to 30%)

Gambellara VENETO, ITA Garganega 80% (other local non-aromatic white varieties 20% max)

Garda LOMBARDY & VENETO, ITA Riesling and/or Riesling Italico 70% min, (other local non-aromatic white varieties 15% max). The following varietal wines are also made: Chardonnay, Cortese, Garganega, Pinot Grigio, Riesling, Riesling Italico, Sauvignon Blanc, Tocai Friulano

Garda Colli Mantovani LOMBARDY, ITA Garganega 35% max, Trebbiano Toscano and/or Trebbiano di Soave 35% max, (Chardonnay 15% max, Sauvignon Blanc, Riesling Renano and/or Riesling Italico 15% max). The following varietal wines are also made: Chardonnay, Pinot Bianco, Pinot Grigio, Sauvignon Blanc and *Tocai Italico*

Gavi PIEDMONT, ITA Cortese

Genazzano LATIUM, ITA Malvasia di Candia 50-70%, *Bellone* and/or Bombino 10-30%, other local white varieties 40% max

Gioia del Colle APULIA , ITA Trebbiano Toscano 50%-70%, other local white varieties 30-50%

Givry BURGUNDY, FRA Chardonnay, (Pinot Blanc)

Golfo del Tigullio LIGURIA, ITA Vermentino 20-70%, *Bianchetta Genovese* 20-70%, other local non-aromatic white varieties 40% max. The following varietal wines are also made: *Bianchetta Genovese*, Vermentino

Graciosa PORTUGAL Verdelho, Arinto, *Terrantez*, Malvasia Fina, *Fernão Pires*

Graves BORDEAUX, FRA Sémillon, Sauvignon Blanc, Muscadelle

Graves de Vayres BORDEAUX, FRA Sémillon, Sauvignon Blanc, Muscadelle (*Merlot Blanc*)

Graves Supérieure BORDEAUX, FRA Sémillon, Sauvignon Blanc, Muscadelle

Gravina APULIA , ITA Malvasia, Greco, *Bianco d'Alessano*, (Bombino Bianco, Trebbiano, *Verdeca*)

Greco di Tufo CAMPANIA, ITA Greco 85% min, (Coda di Volpe 15% max)

Gros Plant LOIRE, FRA Folle Blanche

Gros Plant Nantais LOIRE, FRA Folle Blanche

Guardia Sanframondi CAMPANIA, ITA Malvasia 50-70%, Falanghina 20-30%, (other local white varieties 10% max)

Guardiolo CAMPANIA, ITA Malvasia 50-70%, Falanghina 20-30%, (other local white varieties 10% max)

Gutariako Txacoli SPAIN Hondarrabi Zuri

Haut-Poitou LOIRE, FRA Sauvignon Blanc, Chardonnay, Pinot Blanc, (Chenin Blanc)

Hermitage RHÔNE, FRA Marsanne, Roussanne

Hermitage Vin de Palle RHÔNE, FRA Marsanne, Roussanne

Irouléguy SOUTHWEST, FRA *Courbu,* Manseng

Ischia CAMPANIA, ITA *Forastera* 45-70%, *Biancolella* 30-55%, (other local white varieties 15% max)

Jasnières LOIRE, FRA Chenin Blanc

Jerez-Xérès-Sherry SPAIN Palomino, (Pedro Ximénez, Moscatel)

Jumilla SPAIN Airén, Mabaceo, Pedro Ximénez

Jurançon SOUTHWEST, FRA Petit Manseng, Gros Manseng, *Courbu, (Camaralet, Lauzet)*

Jurançon Sec SOUTHWEST, FRA Petit Manseng, Gros Manseng, *Courbu, (Camaralet, Lauzet)*

Kantza GREECE Savatiano

Ladoix BURGUNDY, FRA Chardonnay, (Pinot Blanc)

La Clape, Coteaux du Languedoc LANGUEDOC-ROUSSILLON, FRA Bourboulenc 60% min, (Grenache Blanc, Clairette, Picpoul Blanc, Ugni Blanc, Roussanne, Marsanne, Macabéo, *Rolle, Terret Blanc, Carignan Blanc)*

Lacryma Christi del Vesuvio CAMPANIA, ITA Coda di Volpe and/or *Verdeca* 80%, (Falanghina and/or Greco 20% max)

La Mancha SPAIN Airén, Viura, *Pardillo, Verdoncho*

La Palma SPAIN Malvasía, (*Albillo, Bastardo, Bermejuela, Bujariego, Burrablanca Forastera, Gual,* Listán, Moscatel, Pedro Ximénez, *Sabro,* Torrontés, Verdello)

Lafões PORTUGAL Arinto and/or *Cercial* 85% min, w/ Arinto at 50% min, *Dona Branca,* Sercial, *Rabo de Ovelha*

Lagoa PORTUGAL Arinto and/or *Síria* 70% min, *Manteúdo, Moscatel Graúdo, Perrum, Rabo de Ovelha* and/or Sauvignon Blanc 30% max

Lagos PORTUGAL Arinto, Malvasia Fina and/or *Síria* 70% min, *Manteúdo, Moscatel Graúdo* and/or *Perrum* 30% max

Lamezia CALABRIA, ITA Greco 50% max, Trebbiano Toscano 40% max, other local white varieties 30% min, (Malvasia 20% min)

Langhe PIEDMONT, ITA One or more local non-aromatic white varieties. The following varietal wines are also made: Arneis, Chardonnay, *Favorita*

Lanzarote SPAIN Malvasía, (*Breval, Burrablanca, Diego,* Listán, Moscatel, Pedro Ximénez)

L'Étoile JURA, FRA Savagnin, *Poulsard,* Chardonnay

L'Étoile Vin Jaune JURA, FRA Savagnin, *Poulsard,* Chardonnay

Lemnos / Limnos GREECE Moschato Alexandreias

Lessini Durello VENETO, ITA *Durello* 85%, (Garganega, Trebbiano di Soave, Pinot Bianco, Pinot Nero and/or Chardonnay 15%)

Leverano APULIA, ITA Malvasia 50% min, Bombino Bianco 40% max, other local white varieties 30% max

Liebfraumilch GERMANY Riesling, Müller-Thurgau, Silvaner, Kerner

Lirac RHÔNE, FRA Grenache Blanc, Clairette, Bourbolenc, (Ugni Blanc, Roussanne, Marsanne, Viognier, Picpoul Blanc)

Lison-Pramaggiore VENETO/FRIULI-VENEZIA GIULIA, ITA Tocai Friulano 50-70%, other local non-aromatic varieties 50% max. The following varietal wines are also made: Chardonnay, Pinot Blanc, Pinot Grigio, Riesling, Sauvignon Blanc, Tocai, *Lison, Verduzzo*

Lizzano APULIA, ITA Trebbiano Toscano 40-60%, Chardonnay and/or Pinot Bianco 30% min, Malvasia, Sauvignon Blanc, *Bianco di Alessano* 25% max

Locorotondo APULIA, ITA *Verdeca* 50-65%, *Bianco d'Alessano* 35-50%, (Fiano, Bombino Bianco, Malvasia 5% max)

Lugana LOMBARDY/VENETO, ITA Trebbiano di Lugana 90% min (other local non-aromatic white varieties 10% max)

Mâcon or Mâcon followed by village name (ie Mâcon-Burgy, Mâcon-Chardonnay, etc) BURGUNDY, FRA Chardonnay, (Pinot Blanc)

Mâcon Supérieur BURGUNDY, FRA Chardonnay, (Pinot Blanc)

Mâcon-Villages BURGUNDY, FRA Chardonnay, (Pinot Blanc)

Malvasia di Bosa SARDINIA, ITA Malvasia di Bosa

Malvasia di Cagliari SARDINIA, ITA Malvasia di Sardegna

Manchuela SPAIN *Albillo,* Mabaceo, Chardonnay, Sauvignon Blanc

Mantinia GREECE *Moschofilero* 85% min, *Asproúdes*

Manzanilla de Sanlúcar de Barrameda SPAIN Palomino, (Pedro Ximénez, Moscatel)

Maranges BURGUNDY, FRA Chardonnay

Marino LATIUM, ITA Malvasia di Candia 60% max, Trebbiano Toscano, Trebbiano Romagnolo, Trebbiano Giallo and/or Trebbiano di Soave 25-55%, Malvasia del Lazio 5-45%, (other local non-aromatic white varieties 10% max)

Marsannay BURGUNDY, FRA Chardonnay, (Pinot Blanc)

Martina (Franca) APULIA, ITA *Verdeca* 50-65%, *Bianco d'Alessano* 35-50%, (Fiano, Bombino Bianco, Malvasia 5% max)

Melissa CALABRIA, ITA Greco 80-95%, (Trebbiano Toscano, Malvasia 5-20%)

Menetou-Salon LOIRE, FRA Sauvignon Blanc

Menfi SICILY, ITA Inzolia, Chardonnay, Catarratto and/or *Grecanico* 75% min, other local non-aromatic white varieties 25% max. The following varietal wines are also made: Chardonnay, *Grecanico*

Mercurey BURGUNDY, FRA Chardonnay

Merlara VENETO, ITA Tocai Friulano 50-70%, other local non-aromatic varieties 50% max. The following varietal wines are also made: Malvasia, Tocai Fruilano

Meursault BURGUNDY, FRA Chardonnay, (Pinot Blanc)

Minervois LANGUEDOC-ROUSSILLON, FRA Grenache Blanc, Bourboulenc, Macabéo, Marsanne, Roussanne, Vermentino, (Picpoul Blanc, Clairette, *Terret Blanc*, Muscat Blanc)

Molise MOLISE, ITA The following varietal wines are also made: Chardonnay, Falanghina, Greco Bianco, Pinot Blanc, Sauvignon Blanc, Trebbiano

Mondéjar SPAIN *Malvar*, Macabeo, Torrontés (Pedro Ximénez)

Monferrato PIEDMONT, ITA One or more local non-aromatic white varieties. The following varietal wine is also made: Cortese

Monreale SICILY, ITA Catarratto and Ansonica/Inzolia 50%, other local white varieties 50% max. The following varietal wines are also made: Ansonica/Inzolia, Catarratto, Chardonnay, *Grillo*, Pinot Bianco

Montagny BURGUNDY, FRA Chardonnay

Montecarlo TUSCANY, ITA Trebbiano Toscano 40-60%, Semillion, Pinot Grigio, Pinot Bianco, Vermentino, Sauvignon Blanc and/or Roussanne 40-60%, (other local white varieties 20% max)

Montecompatri Colonna LATIUM, ITA Malvasia di Candia and/or Puntinata 70% max, Trebbiano Toscano, Trebbiano Verde and/or Trebbiano Giallo 30%, (*Bellone* and/or *Bonvino* 10% max)

Montecucco TUSCANY, ITA Trebbiano Toscano 60% min, other local white varieties 40% max. The following varietal wine is also made: Vermentino

Montefalco UMBRIA, ITA Grechetto 50%, Trebbiano Toscano, 20-35%, (other local non-aromatic white varieties 15% max)

Montello e Colli Asolani VENETO, ITA The following varietal wines are also made: Chardonnay, Pinot Bianco, Pinot Grigio, Prosecco

Monteregio di Massa Marittima TUSCANY, ITA Trebbiano Toscano 50% min, Vermentino, Malvasia Bianca, Malvasia di Candia and/or *Ansonica* 30% max, other local white varieties 30% max. The following varietal wine is also made: Vermentino

Monterrei SPAIN *Doña Blanca, Treixadura* and/or Godello 65% min (Palomino Fino)

Montescudaio TUSCANY, ITA Trebbiano Toscano 50% min, other local white varieties 50% max. The following varietal wines are also made: Chardonnay, Sauvignon Blanc, Vermentino

Monthélie BURGUNDY, FRA Chardonnay, (Pinot Blanc)

Monti Lessini VENETO, ITA Chardonnay 50% min, Pinot Bianco, Pinot Nero, Pinot Grigio and/or Sauvignon Blanc 50% max

Montilla-Moriles SPAIN Pedro Ximénez, Moscatel, (Airén, *Baladí*, Torrontés)

Montlouis LOIRE, FRA Chenin Blanc

Montrachet BURGUNDY, FRA Chardonnay

Montravel SOUTHWEST, FRA Sémillon, Sauvignon Blanc, Muscadelle, Ondenc, Chenin Blanc, Ugni Blanc

Morey-St.-Denis BURGUNDY, FRA Chardonnay

Muscadet LOIRE, FRA Melon de Bourgogne

Muscadet Côtes de Grand Lieu LOIRE, FRA Melon de Bourgogne

Muscadet des Coteaux de la Loire LOIRE, FRA Melon de Bourgogne

Muscadet de Sèvre-et-Maine LOIRE, FRA Melon de Bourgogne

Muscadet Sur Lie LOIRE, FRA Melon de Bourgogne

Musigny BURGUNDY, FRA Chardonnay

Nasco di Cagliari SARDINIA, ITA *Nasco* 100%

Navarra SPAIN Viura, Moscatel, (Chardonnay, Malvasía, Garnacha Blanca)

Nuit-St-Georges BURGUNDY, FRA Chardonnay, (Pinot Blanc)

Nuragus di Cagliari SARDINIA, ITA *Nuragus* 85% (other local white varieties 15% max)

Óbidos PORTUGAL Arinto, *Fernão Pires, Rabo de Ovelha, Seara Nova* and/or *Vital* 70% min, *Alicante Branco*, Chardonnay, Malvasia Rei and/or *Ratinho* 30% max

Offida Passerina MARCHES, ITA *Passerina* 85% (other local non-aromatic white varieties 15% max)

Offida Pecorino MARCHES, ITA *Pecorino* 85% (other local non-aromatic white varieties 15% max)

Oltrepo Pavese LOMBARDY, ITA The following varietal wines are also made: Chardonnay, Cortese, Malvasia, Moscato, Pinot Grigio, Riesling Italico, Riesling Renano, Sauvignon Blanc

Orcia TUSCANY, ITA Trebbiano Toscano 50%, other local non-aromatic white varieties 50% max

Orvieto UMBRIA & LATIUM, ITA Trebbiano Toscano 40-60%, Verdello 15-25%, (Grechetto, Canaiolo and/or Malvasia Toscana 20%, other local white varieties 15% max)

Ostuni APULIA, ITA *Impigno* 50-85%, *Francavilla* 15-50%, (*Bianco Alessano* and/or *Verdeca* 10% max)

Pacherenc du Vic-Bilh SOUTHWEST, FRA *Arrufiac, Courbu*, Gros Manseng, Petit Manseng, (Sauvignon Blanc, Sémillon)

Pagadebit di Romagna EMILIA-ROMAGNA, ITA Bombino Bianco 85%, other local white varieties 15% max

Palette PROVENCE, FRA Clairette, (*Picardin*, Ugni Blanc, *Ugni Rosé,* Grenache Blanc, Muscat, Picpoul Blanc, *Pascal, Aragnan,* Colombard, *Terret-Bourret*)

Palmela PORTUGAL Arinto, *Fernão Pires, Moscatel Galego Branco, Moscatel Graúdo, Moscatel Galego Roxo*, Rabo de Ovelha, *Síria, Tamarez* and/or *Vital*

Parrina TUSCANY, ITA Trebbiano Toscano 30-50%, Inzolia and/or Chardonnay 30-50%, (other local white varieties 20% max)

Patras / Pátra GREECE Roditis

Patrimonio CORSICA, FRA Vermentino

Penedés SPAIN Macabeo, Xarel-lo, (Parellada, *Malvasía Riojana*, Gewürztraminer, Riesling, Muscat Ottonel, Chenin Blanc, Chardonnay, Sauvignon Blanc)

Penisola Sorrentina CAMPANIA, ITA *Biancolella,* Falanghina and/or Greco 60%, other local white varieties 40% max

Pentro di Isernia MOLISE, ITA Trebbiano Toscano 60-70%, Bombino Bianco 30-40% (other local white varieties 10%)

Pernard-Vergelesses BURGUNDY, FRA Chardonnay, (Pinot Blanc)

Pessac-Léognan BORDEAUX, FRA Sémillon, Sauvignon Blanc, (Muscadelle)

Petite Chablis BURGUNDY, FRA Chardonnay

Pezá GREECE Vilána

Piave VENETO, ITA Chardonnay, Pinot Blanc, Pinot Grigio, *Tocai Italico*, *Verduzzo*

Picpoul-de-Pinet, Coteaux du Languedoc LANGUEDOC-ROUSSILLON, FRA Picpoul Blanc

Piemonte PIEDMONT, ITA The following varietal wines are also made: Chardonnay, Cortese

Pla de Bagés SPAIN Macabeo, Parellada, Chardonnay, *Picapoll*

Pla i llevant SPAIN Macabeo, Parellada, Chardonnay, *Prensal Blanco,* (Moscatel)

Planalto Mirandês PORTUGAL *Gouveio*, Malvasia Fina, *Rabigato* and/or *Viosinho* 60% min (other local varieties 40% max)

Pomino TUSCANY, ITA Pinot Bianco and/or Chardonnay 60-80%, Trebbiano Toscano 30% max (other local white varieties 15% max)

Portimão PORTUGAL Arinto and/or *Síria* 70% min, *Manteúdo, Moscatel Graúdo, Perrum* and/or *Rabo de Ovelha* 30% max

Pouilly-Fuissé BURGUNDY, FRA Chardonnay

Pouilly-Fumé LOIRE, FRA Sauvignon Blanc

Pouilly-Loché BURGUNDY, FRA Chardonnay

Pouilly-sur-Loire LOIRE, FRA Chasselas, (Sauvignon Blanc)

Pouilly-Vinzelles BURGUNDY, FRA Chardonnay

Premières Côtes de Blaye BORDEAUX, FRA Sémillon, Sauvignon Blanc, Muscadelle

Priorato SPAIN Garnacha Blanca, Macabeo, Pedro Ximénez

Prosecco di Conegliano-Valdobbiadene VENETO, ITA Prosecco 85%, (*Verdisio, Bianchetta, Perera* and/or Prosecco Lungo 15% max)

Puligny-Montrachet BURGUNDY, FRA Chardonnay, (Pinot Blanc)

Quincy LOIRE, FRA Sauvignon Blanc

Ramandolo FRIULI-VENEZIA GIULIA, ITA *Verduzzo Friulano*

Reno EMILIA-ROMAGNA, ITA *Albana* and/or Trebbiano Romagnolo 40%, other local non-aromatic white varieties 60%. The following varietal wines are also made: *Montuni, Pignoletto*

Retsina GREECE Savatiano, (Rhoditis, Assyrtiko)

Reuilly LOIRE, FRA Sauvignon Blanc

Rhodes / Ródos GREECE *Athiri*

Rías Baixas SPAIN Albariño, (*Treixadura*, Loureiro, *Caiño Blanco*, Torrontés)

Ribatejo PORTUGAL Arinto, *Fernão Pires, Rabo de Ovelha, Tália,* Trincadeira, Verdelho and/or *Vital* 50% min, *Alicante Branco,* Alvarinho, *Cerceal Branco,* Chardonnay, Malvasia Rei, *Moscatel Graúdo,* Pinot Blanc, Sauvignon Blanc, *Síria, Tamarez, Viosinho* 50% max

Ribeira Sacra SPAIN Loureiro, Godello, Albariño, *Doña Blanca,* Torrontés, *Treixadura* (Palomino)

Ribera del Guadiana SPAIN *Pardina,* Cayetana Blanca, Macabeo, *Alarije, Borba,* Chardonnay, *Montúa, Eva, Malvar,* Parellada, Pedro Ximénez, Verdejo

Rioja SPAIN Viura, Malvasía, (Garnacha Blanca)

Riviera del Garda Bresciano LOMBARDY, ITA Riesling Renano and/or Riesling Italico 80%, (other local white varieties 20%)

Riviera Ligure di Ponente LIGURIA, ITA The following varietal wines are made: Pigato, Vermentino

Robóla of Cephalonia / Kefalonia GREECE *Robola*

Roussette du Bugey SAVOIE, FRA *Roussette,* Chardonnay

Roussette du Savoie SAVOIE, FRA *Roussette, Monduese,* Chardonnay

Rueda SPAIN Verdejo and/or Sauvignon Blanc 50% min, Macabeo and/or Palomino 50% max

Rueda Superior SPAIN Verdejo 85% min, (Sauvignon Blanc, Macabeo and/or Palomino 15% max)

Rully BURGUNDY, FRA Chardonnay

St.-Aubin BURGUNDY, FRA Chardonnay, (Pinot Blanc)

Ste-Foy-Bordeaux BORDEAUX, FRA Sémillon, Sauvignon Blanc, Muscadelle, (*Merlot Blanc*, Columbard, Mauzac, Ugni Blanc 10% max)

St.-Joseph RHÔNE, FRA Marsanne, Roussanne

St.-Péray RHÔNE, FRA Marsanne, Roussanne

Saint-Pourçain LOIRE, FRA *Tressallier, St.Pierre-Doré,* Aligoté, Chardonnay, Sauvignon Blanc

St.-Romain BURGUNDY, FRA Chardonnay, (Pinot Blanc)

St.-Véran BURGUNDY, FRA Chardonnay

Salice Salentino PUGLIA, ITA Chardonnay 70% min, Pinot Bianco and/or other local white varieties 30% max

Sambuca di Sicilia SICILY, ITA Ansonica 50-100%, other local non-aromatic white varieties 50% max. The following varietal wines are also made: Ansonica, Chardonnay, *Grecanico*

San Colombano al Lambro LOMBARDY, ITA Chardonnay 50-90%, Pinot Nero 10-50%

Sancerre LOIRE, FRA Sauvignon Blanc

San Martino della Battaglia LOMBARDY/VENETO, ITA Tocai Friulano 80%, (other local white varieties 20% max)

Sannio CAMPANIA, ITA Trebbiano, 50% min, other local white varieties, 50% max. The following varietal wines are also made: Coda di Volpe, Falanghina, Fiano, Greco

San Severo PUGLIA, ITA Bombino Bianco 40-60%, Trebbiano 40-60%, (Malvasia and/or *Verdeca* 20% max)

Sant'Agata dei Goti CALABRIA, ITA Falanghina 40-60%, Greco 40-60%, other local white varieties 20% max

Sant'Antimo TUSCANY, ITA One or more local white varieties 100%. The following varietal wines are also made: Chardonnay, Pinot Grigio, Sauvignon Blanc

Santa Margherita di Belice SICILY, ITA Ansonica 30-50%, *Grecanico* and/or Catarratto Lucido 50-70%, (other local white varieties 15% max). The following varietal wines are also made: Ansonica, Catarratto, *Grecanico*

Santenay BURGUNDY, FRA Chardonnay, (Pinot Blanc)

Santorini GREECE Assyrtiko, (*Aidáni Aspro, Athíiri*)

San Vito di Luzzi CALABRIA, ITA Malvasia 40-60%, Greco 20-30%, other local white varieties 30% max

Sardegna Semidano SARDINIA, ITA *Semidano* 85% (other local white varieties 15% max)

Saumur LOIRE, FRA Chenin Blanc 80% min, (Chardonnay, Sauvignon Blanc)

Savennières LOIRE, FRA Chenin Blanc

Savennières Coulée-de-Serrant LOIRE, FRA Chenin Blanc

Savennières Roche-aux-Moines LOIRE, FRA Chenin Blanc

Savigny-lès-Beaune BURGUNDY, FRA Chardonnay, (Pinot Blanc)

Scavigna CALABRIA, ITA Trebbiano 50% max, Chardonnay 30% max, other local white varieties 35% max, (Greco 20% max, Malvasia 10% max)

Sciacca SICILY, ITA Inzolia, *Grecanico*, Chardonnay and/or Catarratto 70%, other local non-aromatic white varieties 30% max. The following varietal wines are also made: *Grecanico*, Inzolia

Sciacca Riserva Rayana SICILY, ITA Catarratto and/or Inzolia 80% (other local non-aromatic white varieties 20% max)

Seyssel SAVOIE, FRA *Roussette*

Sitía GREECE Vilána 70% min, *Thrapsathíri*

Soave VENETO, ITA Garganega 70-100%, Pinot Bianco, Chardonnay and/or Trebbiano di Soave 30% max (other local non-aromatic white varieties 5% max)

Solopaca CALABRIA, ITA TrebbianoToscano 40-60%, Falanghina, Coda di Volpe, Malvasia Toscana and/or Malvasia di Candia 60% max, (other local white varieties 20% max). The following varietal wine is also made: Falanghina

Somontano SPAIN Macabeo, Garnacha Blanca, *Alcañon*, Chardonnay

Taburno CAMPANIA, ITA Trebbiano Toscano 40-50%, Falanghina 30-40%, other local white varieties 30% max. The following varietal wines are also made: Coda di Volpe, Falanghina, Greco

Tacoronte-Acentejo SPAIN Listán Blanca, *Gual*, Verdello, Malvasía, Moscatel, *Vijariego*

Tarquinia LATIUM, ITA Trebbiano 50%, Malvasia di Candia and/or Malvasia del Lazio 35% max, other local white varieties except Pinot Grigio 30% max

Tarragona SPAIN Mabaceo, Xarel-lo, Parellada, Garnacha Blanca

Tavira PORTUGAL Arinto and/or *Síria* 70% max, *Diagalves, Manteúdo, Moscatel Graúdo* and/or *Tamarez* 30% max

Távora-Varosa PORTUGAL Bical, Arinto, Chardonnay, *Dona Branca*, Fernão *Pires, Folgasão, Gouveio*, Malvasia Fina 30% min for new producers, Malvasia Rei 10% max, *Rabo de Ovelha, Síria, Viosinho*

Terra Alta SPAIN Garnacha Blanca, Macabeo, Parellada, Moscatel

Terre di Franciacorta LOMBARDY, ITA Pinot Bianco, Chardonnay and/or Pinot Nero 100%

Tokaji Szamorodni HUNGARY Furmint, Hársevelü, (Muscat Blanc, *Orémus*)

Torgiano UMBRIA, ITA, Trebbiano Toscano 50-70%, Grechetto 15-40% (other local white varieties 15%). The following varietal wines are also made: Chardonnay, Pinot Grigio, Riesling Italico

Toro SPAIN Malvasía, (Verdejo)

Torres Vedras PORTUGAL Arinto, *Fernão Pires, Rabo de Ovelha, Seara Nova*, and/or *Vital* 70% min, *Alicante Branco*, Alvarinho, *Antão Vaz*, Chardonnay, Malvasia Rei, Sauvignon Blanc and/or *Viosinho* 30% max

Touraine LOIRE, FRA Sauvignon Blanc, (Chenin Blanc, *Arbois*, Chardonnay)

Touraine-Amboise LOIRE, FRA Chenin Blanc

Touraine Azay-le-Rideau LOIRE, FRA Chenin Blanc

Touraine-Mesland LOIRE, FRA Chenin Blanc

Trebbiano d'Abruzzo ABRUZZI, ITA Bombino Bianco and/or Trebbiano Toscano 85%, (other local white varieties 15% max)

Trebbiano di Romagna EMILIA-ROMAGNA, ITA Trebbiano Romagnolo 85-100% (other local white varieties 15% max)

Trentino TRENTINO-ALTO ADIGE, ITA Chardonnay and/or Pinot Bianco 80-100%, (Sauvignon Blanc, Müller-Thurgau and/or *Manzoni Bianco* 20% max). The following varietal wines are also made: Chardonnay, Müller-Thurgau, Pinot Grigio, Riesling, Riesling Italico, Sauvignon Blanc, Traminer Aromatico. Also, blended white varietal wines are made from Chardonnay, Pinot Bianco, Pinot Grigio and Sauvignon Blanc with the first variety in the name 51-75%, and the second variety 25-49%

Trentino Sorni TRENTINO-ALTO ADIGE, ITA *Nosiola*, Müller Thurgau, Silvaner Verde, Pinot Bianco, Pinot Grigio and/or Chardonnay 100%

Trentino Superiore TRENTINO-ALTO ADIGE, ITA Chardonnay, Pinot Bianco and/or Pinot Grigio 85-100%, (Sauvignon Blanc, Traminer, Riesling and/or *Manzoni Bianco* 15% max)

Tursan SOUTHWEST, FRA *Baroque* 90% min, (Sauvignon Blanc, Gros Manseng, Petit Manseng, *Claverie, Cruchinet, Raffiat, Claret du Gers*, Clairette)

Utiel-Requena SPAIN Macabeo, *Merseguera*, (*Planta Nova*)

Utiel-Requena Superior SPAIN Macabeo

Vacqueyras RHÔNE, FRA Grenache Blanc, Clairette, Bourboulenc, Marsanne, Roussanne, Viognier

Val d'Arbia TUSCANY, ITA, Trebbiano Toscano and/or Malvasia del Chianti 70-90%, Chardonnay 10-30%

Val di Cornia TUSCANY, ITA Trebbiano Toscano 60% min, Vermentino 50% max (other local white varieties 20% max) The following varietal wines are also made: *Ansonica*, Vermentino

Val Polcevera LIGURIA, ITA Vermentino, *Bianchetta, Genovese* and/or *Albarola* 60% min, Pigato, *Rollo* and/or *Bosco* 40% max. The following varietal wines are also made: *Bianchetta Genovese*, Vermentino

Valcalepio LOMBARDY, ITA Pinot Bianco and/or Chardonnay 55-80%, Pinot Grigio 20-45%

Valdadige VENETO / TRENTINO-ALTO ADIGE, ITA Trebbiano Toscano, *Nosiola*, Sauvignon Blanc and/or Garganega 20-80%, Pinot Bianco, Pinot Grigio, Riesling Italico, Chardonnay and/or Müller Thurgau 20-80%. The following varietal wines are also made: Chardonnay, Pinot Bianco, Pinot Grigio

Valdeorras SPAIN Palomino, Godello, *Doña Blanca*

Valdepeñas SPAIN Airén, (Macabeo, Chardonnay)

Valdichiana Bianco Vergine TUSCANY, ITA Trebbiano Toscano 20%, Chardonnay, Pinot Bianco, Grechetto and/or Pinot Grigio 80% max (other local non-aromatic white varieties 15% max). The following varietal wines are also made: Chardonnay, Grechetto

Valençay LOIRE, FRA *Arbois*, Chardonnay, Chenin Blanc, Sauvignon Blanc, *Romorantin*

Valencia SPAIN Macabeo, Malvasía, *Merseguera*, Moscatel de Alejandría, Pedro Ximénez, *Planta Fina de Pedralba, Planta Nova, Tortosí*

Valle d'Aosta AOSTA, ITA One or more local varieties. The following varietal wines are also made: Chardonnay, Müller Thurgau, Petite Arvine, Pinot Bianco, Pinot Grigio

Valle d'Aosta Blanc de Morgex et de la Salle AOSTA, ITA *Prié*

Valle d'Aosta Chambave Moscato AOSTA, ITA Moscato

Valle d'Aosta Nus Malvoisie LATIUM, ITA Pinot Grigio

Valle de Güímar SPAIN Palomino, *Forestera*, (Malvasía, *Güal, Vijariego*)

Valle de la Orotava SPAIN Listán Blanco, (*Bastardo Blanco, Güal, Forastera Blanca*, Malvasía, *Marmajuelo*, Moscatel, Pedro Ximénez, Torrontés, Verdello, *Vijariego*)

Valpaços PORTUGAL *Roupeiro, Fernão Pires*, Gouveio and/or Malvasia Fina 70% min (other local varieties 30% max)

Velletri LATIUM, ITA Malvasia di Candia and/or Malvasia Puntinata 70% max, Trebbiano 30%, (*Bellone*, Bombino Bianco and/or other local white varieties 20% max)

Verbicaro CALABRIA, ITA Greco, Malvasia and/or *Guarnaccia Bianca* 70% min, other local white varieties 30% max

Verdicchio dei Castelli di Iesi MARCHES, ITA Verdicchio 85% min, (Malvasia Toscana and/or Trebbiano 15% max)

Verdicchio di Matelica MARCHES, ITA Verdicchio 85% min, (Malvasia Toscana and/or Trebbiano 15% max)

Vermentino di Gallura SARDINIA, ITA Vermentino 95-100%, other local white varieties 5% max

Vermentino di Sardegna SARDINIA, ITA Vermentino 85%, (other local white varieties 15% max)

Vernaccia di San Gimignano TUSCANY, ITA Vernaccia 90% min, other local white varieties 10% max

Vernaccia di Oristano SARDINIA, ITA Vernaccia di Oristano

Vesuvio CAMPANIA, ITA Coda di Volpe and/or *Verdeca* 80%, (Falanghina and/or Greco 20% max)

Vicenza VENETO, ITA Garganega 50%, other local non-aromatic white varieties 50%. The following varietal wines are also made: Chardonnay, Garganega, *Manzoni Bianco*, Pinot Bianco, Riesling, Sauvignon Blanc

Vignanello LATIUM, ITA Trebbiano Giallo and/or Trebbiano Toscano 60-70%, Malvasia di Candia and/or Malvasia del Chianti 20-40%, (other local white varieties 10%). The following varietal wine is also made: Greco

Vin du Bugey SAVOIE, FRA Chardonnay, *Roussette*, Aligoté, *Mondeuse Blanc, Jacquère*, Pinot Gris, *Molette*

Vin de Corse CORSICA, FRA Vermentino 75% min, (Ugni Blanc)

Vin du Savoie SAVOIE, FRA Aligoté, Chardonnay, *Jacquère, Roussette, Mondeuse Blanc,* Malvoisie, (Chasselas, *Gringet, Roussette d'Ayze,* Marsanne, *Verdesse*)

Vinho Verde PORTUGAL Alvarinho, Arinto, Avesso, *Azal, Batoca*, Loureiro, *Trajadura*

Vinos de Madrid SPAIN *Malvar, Albillo*, Airén

Vin Santo del Chianti TUSCANY, ITA Trebbiano Toscano and/or Malvasia 70%, other local varieties 30% max

Vin Santo del Chianti Classico TUSCANY, ITA Trebbiano Toscano and/or Malvasia 70%, other local varieties 30% max

Vin Santo di Montepulciano TUSCANY, ITA Malvasia Bianca, Grechetto, and/or Trebbiano Toscano 70%, other local white varieties 30% max

Vins de l'Orléanais LOIRE, FRA Chardonnay, Pinot Gris

Vins d'Entraygues et du Fel SOUTHWEST, FRA Mauzac, Chenin Blanc

Vins d'Estaing SOUTHWEST, FRA Chenin Blanc, *Roussellou*, Mauzac

Vins de Lavilledieu SOUTHWEST, FRA Mauzac, Chenin Blanc, Sémillon, Muscadelle, Colombard, *Ondenc,* Folle Blanche

Vins du Thouarsais LOIRE, FRA Chenin Blanc 80% min, (Chardonnay)

Vougeot BURGUNDY, FRA Chardonnay, (Pinot Blanc)

Vouvray LOIRE, FRA Chenin Blanc (*Arbois*)

Ycoden-Daute-Isora SPAIN Listán Blanco, (*Bastardo, Bermejuela, Forastera, Gual,* Malvasía, Moscatel, Pedro Ximénez, *Sabro,* Torrontés, Verdello, *Vijariego*)

Yecla SPAIN *Merseguera,* Macabeo, Airén, (Sauvignon Blanc)

Zagarolo LATIUM, ITA Malvasia di Candia and/or Puntinata 70% max, Trebbiano 30%, (*Bellone* and/or *Bonvino* 10% max)

Zítsa GREECE *Debína*

ROSÉ WINES

Ajaccio CORSICA, FRA *Sciacarello, Barbarossa, Nielluccio,* Vermentino, (Grenache, Cinsaut, Carignan)

Aglianico del Taburno CAMPANIA, ITA Aglianico 85%, (other local red varieties 15% max)

Albugnano PIEDMONT, ITA Nebbiolo 85% (Freisa, Barbera and/or Bonarda, 15% max)

Alcamo SICILY, ITA Nerello Mascalese, Nero d'Avola, Sangiovese, Frappato, *Perricone*, Cabernet Sauvignon, Merlot and/or Syrah

Alella SPAIN Tempranillo, Garnacha, (Garnacha Peluda, Cabernet Sauvignon, Merlot, Pinot Noir)

Alezio APULIA , ITA Negroamaro 80% min, (*Malvasia Nera*, Montepulciano, Sangiovese)

Alghero SARDINIA, ITA One or more local non-aromatic red varieties 100%

Alicante SPAIN Monastrell, Bobal, Garnacha (Garnacha Tintorera, Tempranillo, Cabernet Sauvignon, Merlot, Syrah, Pinot Noir)

Almansa SPAIN Monastrell, Tempranillo, Garnacha Tintorera

Ampurdán-Costa Brava SPAIN Cariñena, Garnacha, Tempranillo, Cabernet Sauvignon, Merlot, (Syrah)

Anjou LOIRE, FRA Grolleau, (Cabernet Franc, Cabernet Sauvignon, Pineau d'Aunis, Gamay, Malbec)

Anjou Pétillant LOIRE, FRA Grolleau, (Cabernet Franc, Cabernet Sauvignon, Pineau d'Aunis, Gamay, Malbec)

Arbois JURA, FRA *Poulsard, Trousseau*, Pinot Noir

Arbois Pupillin JURA, FRA *Poulsard, Trousseau*, Pinot Noir

Assisi UMBRIA, ITA Sangiovese 50-70%, Merlot 10-30%, other local red varieties 40% max

Bagnoli (di Sopra) VENETO, ITA *Raboso Piave* and/or *Raboso Veronese* 50% min, Merlot 40% max, other local non-aromatic white varieties 10% max

Bairrada PORTUGAL Baga, Alfrocheiro, *Camarate*, Castelão, *Jaén* and/or Touriga Nacional 85% min w/ Baga at 50% min, (Aragonez, *Bastardo*, Cabernet Sauvignon, Merlot, Pinot Noir, *Rufete*, Syrah, Tinta Barroca, Tinto Cão, Touriga Franca)

Bandol PROVENCE, FRA Mourvèdre, (Grenache, Cinsaut, Syrah, Carignan)

Bardolino VENETO, ITA Corvina 35-65%, Rondinella 10-40%, (Molinara 10-20%, *Negrara* 10%, *Rossignola*, Barbera, Sangiovese, Garganega 15% max)

Béarn SOUTHWEST, FRA Tannat, (Cabernet Sauvignon, Cabernet Franc, Fer, *Manseng Noir, Courbu Noir*)

Beaujolais BURGUNDY, FRA Gamay (Pinot Noir, Pinot Gris)

Beaujolais-Villages BURGUNDY, FRA Gamay (Pinot Noir, Pinot Gris)

Bellet PROVENCE, FRA Braquet, *Fuella,* Cinsaut, (Grenache, *Rolle*, Ugni Blanc, *Mayorquin,* Clairette, Bourboulenc, Chardonnay, *Pignerol,* Muscat Blanc)

Bergerac SOUTHWEST, FRA Cabernet Sauvignon, Cabernet Franc, Merlot, (Malbec, Fer, *Mérille*)

Bierzo SPAIN *Doña Mencía* 50% min (Garnacha Tintorera, Cabernet Sauvignon, Merlot, Pinot Noir, Tempranillo)

Biferno MOLISES, ITA Montepulciano 60-70%, (Trebbiano Toscano 15-20%, Aglianico 15-20%, other local varieties 5% max)

Binissalem SPAIN *Manto Negro*, Callet, Tempranillo, Monastrell

Bivongi CALABRIA, ITA Gaglioppo and/or *Greco Nero* 30-50%, *Nocera* and/or Calabrese 30-50%, (other local red varieties 10% max, other local white varieties 15% max)

Bolgheri TUSCANY, ITA Cabernet Sauvignon 10-80%, Merlot 80% max, Sangiovese 70% max, other local red varieties 30% max

Bolgheri Sassicaia TUSCANY, ITA Cabernet Sauvignon 10-80%, Merlot 80% max, Sangiovese 70% max, other local red varieties 30% max

Bordeaux BORDEAUX, FRA Cabernet Sauvignon, Cabernet Franc, Merlot, (Malbec, Petit Verdot, Carmenère)

Bordeaux Supérieur BORDEAUX, FRA Cabernet Sauvignon, Cabernet Franc, Merlot, (Malbec, Petit Verdot, Carmenère)

Bourgogne BURGUNDY, FRA Pinot Noir, Pinot Gris, Pinot Liébault, (*César, Tressot*)

Bourgogne Hauts-Côtes de Nuits BURGUNDY, FRA Pinot Noir, Pinot Gris, Pinot Liébault

Bourgogne Grand-Ordinaire BURGUNDY, FRA Pinot Noir, Gamay (*César, Tressot*)

Bourgogne Passetoutgrains BURGUNDY, FRA Pinot Noir, Pinot Liébault. Gamay 33% max

Bourgueil LOIRE, FRA Cabernet Franc 90-100%, (Cabernet Sauvignon)

Brindisi APULIA, ITA Negroamaro 70%, (Montepulciano, Malvasia Nera, Sangiovese, *Susumaniello*)

Bullas SPAIN Monastrell

Buzet SOUTHWEST, FRA Merlot, Cabernet Sauvignon, Cabernet Franc, Malbec

Cabardès LANGUEDOC-ROUSSILLON, FRA Cinsaut, Grenache, Syrah, (Merlot, Cabernet Sauvignon, Cabernet Franc, Malbec, Fer)

Cabernet d'Anjou LOIRE, FRA Cabernet Franc, (Cabernet Sauvignon)

Cabernet de Saumur LOIRE, FRA Cabernet Franc, (Cabernet Sauvignon)

Calatayud SPAIN Garnacha, Mazuelo, Tempranillo, (Monastrel, Cabernet Sauvignon, Syrah)

Campo de Borja SPAIN Garnacha, Tempranillo, (Mazuelo, Cabernet Sauvugnon, Merlot, Syrah)

Canavese PIEDMONT, ITA Nebbiolo, Barbera, Bonarda, Freisa and/or *Neretto* 60% min, other local red varieties 40% max

Cannonau di Sardegna SARDINIA, ITA Grenache 90%, (other local red varieties 10% max)

Capalbio TUSCANY, ITA Sangiovese 50% min (other local non-aromatic red varieties 50% max)

Cariñena SPAIN Garnacha, Tempranillo, (Cariñena, *Juan Ibáñez*, Monsatrell, Cabernet Sauvignon)

Carmignano TUSCANY, ITA Sangiovese 50%, Canaiolo 20%, (Cabernet Franc and/or Cabernet Sauvignon 10-20%, Trebbiano, *Canaiolo Bianco* and/or Malvasia del Chianti 10% max, other local red varieties 10% max)

Cassis PROVENCE, FRA Grenache, Carignan, Mourvèdre, Cinsaut, *Barbaroux (Terret, Aramon)*

Castel del Monte APULIA , ITA *Bombino Nero* 65% min,

(Uva di Troia, Montepulciano, Aglianico, Pinot Nero)

Castelli Romani LATIUM, ITA *Cesanese*, Merlot, Montepulciano, *Nero Buono*, Sangiovese 100%

Castel San Lorenzo CAMPANIA, ITA Barbera 60-80%, Sangiovese 20-30%, (other local red varieties 20% max)

Cerveteri LATIUM, ITA Sangiovese and/or Montepulciano 60%, *Cesanese* 25%, Canaiolo, Carignano and Barbera 30% max

Châteaumeillant LOIRE, FRA Gamay, (Pinot Gris, Pinot Noir)

Châtillon-en-Diois RHÔNE, FRA Gamay (Syrah, Pinot Noir)

Cheverny LOIRE, FRA Gamay 50% min, (Cabernet Franc, Cabernet Sauvignon, Malbec, Pineau d'Aunis, Pinot Gris)

Chinon LOIRE, FRA Cabernet Franc 75-100% (Cabernet Sauvignon)

Cigales SPAIN Tempranillo 60-80%, (Garnacha 20% max, Verdejo, Viura, Palomino and/or *Albillo* 20% min)

Cilento CAMPANIA, ITA Sangiovese 70-80%, (Aglianico 10-15%, Primitivo and/or Piedirosso 10-15%, other local red varieties 10% max)

Circeo LATIUM, ITA Merlot 85% min, (other local red varieties 15% max)

Cirò CALABRIA, ITA Gaglioppo 95% min, (Trebbiano, Greco)

Colli Altotiberini UMBRIA, ITA Sangiovese 55-70%, (Merlot 10-20%, Trebbiano Toscano and/or Malvasia del Chianti 10%, other local red varieties 15% max)

Colli Amerini UMBRIA, ITA Sangiovese 65-80%, Montepulciano, *Ciliegiolo*, Canaiolo, Merlot and/or Barbera 30% max, (other local red varieties 15% max)

Colli del Trasimeno UMBRIA, ITA Gamay, Cabernet Sauvignon, Merlot and/or Pinot Nero 70%, (Sangiovese 15%, other local red varieties 15% max)

Colli della Sabina LATIUM, ITA Sangiovese 40-70%, Montepulciano 15-40%, other local red varieties 30% max

Colli dell'Etruria Centrale TUSCANY, ITA Sangiovese 50%, Cabernet Franc, Cabernet Sauvignon, Merlot, Pinot Nero or Canaiolo Nero 50% max, other local varieties 25% max

Colli Perugini Umbria, ITA Sangiovese 50% min, other local red varieties 50% max

Colli Pesaresi Marches, ITA Sangiovese 70% min, other local non-aromatic red varieties 30% max

Colli Piacentini EMILIA-ROMAGNA, ITA Pinot Noir

Colli Tortonesi PIEDMONT, ITA One or more local non-aromatic red varieties as a blend. The following varietal wines are also made: Barbera, Dolcetto

Collioure LANGUEDOC-ROUSSILLON, FRA Grenache, Mourvédre, (Carignan, Syrah, Cinsaut, *Grenache Gris*)

Conca de Barberá SPAIN Garnacha, *Trepat*, Tempranillo (Cabernet Sauvignon, Merlot, Pinot Noir)

Contea di Sclafani SICILY, ITA Nerello Mascalese 50%, other local red varieties 50% max

Contessa Entellina SICILY, ITA Nero d'Avola and/or Syrah, 50% min, other local non-aromatic red varieties 50% max

Copertino APULIA, ITA Negroamaro 70% min, (Malvasia Nera, Montepulciano, Sangiovese)

Corbières LANGUEEDOC Carignan 40-60%, (Grenache, Lladoner Pelut, Syrah, Mourvèdre, *Picpoul Noir*, *Terret Noir*, Cinsaut, Macabeo, Bourboulenc)

Cortona TUSCANY, ITA Sangiovese 40-60%, Canaiolo 10-30% (other local non-aromatic red varieties 30% max)

Costa d'Amalfi CAMPANIA, ITA Piedirosso 40%, *Sciascinoso* and/or Aglianico up to 60%, other local red varieties 40% max

Coste della Sesia PIEDMONT, ITA Nebbiolo, Bonarda, *Vespolina*, *Croatina* and/or Barbera 50%, other local non-aromatic red varieties 50% max

Costers del Segre SPAIN Garnacha, Tempranillo, Cabernet Sauvignon, Merlot, Monastrell, *Trepat*, Mazuelo, Pinot Noir

Costières de Nîmes LANGUEDOC-ROUSSILLON, FRA Carignan, Grenache, Mourvédre, Syrah, Cinsaut (Clairette, Bourboulenc, Grenache Blanc, Roussanne, Ugni Blanc, Marsanne)

Coteaux d'Ancenis LOIRE, FRA Gamay, (Cabernet Sauvignon, Cabernet Franc, *Gamay de Chaudenay, Gamay de Bouze*)

Coteaux du Giennois BURGUNDY, FRA Gamay, Pinot Noir

Coteaux du Giennois Cosne-sur-Loire BURGUNDY, FRA Gamay, Pinot Noir

Coteaux du Languedoc LANGUEDOC-ROUSSILLON, FRA Carignan, Grenache, Lladoner Pelut, (Counoise, *Terret Noir*, *Picpoul Noir*, Picpoul Blanc, Bourboulenc, *Carignan Blanc*, Clairette, Macabéo, *Terret Blanc*, Ugni Blanc)

Coteaux de Loir LOIRE, FRA Pinot d'Aunis, Gamay, Cabernet Franc, Malbec, Grolleau

Coteaux du Lyonnais BURGUNDY, FRA Gamay

Coteaux de Pierrevert RHÔNE, FRA Carignan, Grenache, Syrah, Mourvèdre, Cinsaut, (*Terret Noir, Oeillade*)

Coteaux de Tricanstin RHÔNE, FRA Grenache, Syrah, Mourvèdre, Cinsaut, *Picpoul Noir*, (Carignan, Grenache Blanc, Clairette, Bourbolenc, Ugni Blanc)

Coteaux Varois PROVENCE, FRA Grenache, Syrah, Mourvèdre, (Carignan, Cinsaut, Cabernet Sauvignon, *Tibouren*)

Coteaux de Vendômois LOIRE, FRA Pinot d'Aunis 70% min, (Gamay)

Côtes d'Auvergne LOIRE, FRA Gamay, (Pinot Noir)

Côtes du Brulhois SOUTHWEST, FRA Cabernet Sauvignon, Cabernet Franc, Merlot, Malbec, Fer, Tannnat

Côtes de Duras SOUTHWEST, FRA Cabernet Sauvignon, Cabernet Franc, Merlot, Malbec,

Côtes du Forez LOIRE, FRA Gamay

Côtes du Frontonnais SOUTHWEST, FRA Négrette 50-70%, Malbec, Cabernet Sauvignon, Cabernet Franc, *Mérille*, Syrah, Fer, (Gamay, Cinsaut, Mauzac 15% max)

Côtes du Frontonnais Fronton SOUTHWEST, FRA Négrette 50-70%, Malbec, Cabernet Sauvignon, Cabernet Franc, *Mérille*, Syrah, Fer, (Gamay, Cinsaut, Mauzac 15% max)

Côtes du Frontonnais Villaudric SOUTHWEST, FRA Négrette 50-70%, Malbec, Cabernet Sauvignon, Cabernet Franc, *Mérille*, Syrah, Fer, (Gamay, Cinsaut, Mauzac 15% max)

Côtes du Jura JURA, FRA *Poulsard, Trousseau*, Pinot Noir, Pinot Gris, Savagnin, Chardonnay

Côtes du Lubéron RHÔNE, FRA Grenache, Syrah, Mourvèdre, Cinsaut, Carignan, (Grenache Blanc, Clairette, Bourboulenc, Vermentino, Ugni Blanc, Rousanne, Marsanne, *Picpoul Noir*, Pinot Noir, Counoise, Gamay)

Côtes de la Malepère LANGUEDOC-ROUSSILLON, FRA Grenache, Lladoner Pelut, Cinsaut (Merlot, Cabernet Sauvignon, Cabernet Franc, Syrah)

Côtes du Marmandais SOUTHWEST, FRA Cabernet Sauvignon, Cabernet Franc, Merlot 75% max, *Abouriou*, Fer, Gamay, Malbec, Syrah 50% max

Côtes de Millau LANGUEDOC-ROUSSILLON, FRA Gamay, (Syrah, Fer, *Duras,* Cabernet Sauvignon)

Côtes de Provence PROVENCE, FRA Carignan, Cinsaut, Grenache, Mourvèdre, *Tibouren*, (Syrah, Cabernet Sauvignon, *Barbaroux Rosé, Calitor,* Clairette, Sémillon, Ugni Blanc, Vermentino)

Côtes-du-Rhône RHÔNE, FRA Grenache, Clairette, Syrah, Mourvèdre, *Picpoul Noir, Terret Noir, Picardin*, Cinsaut, Roussanne, Marsanne, Bourboulenc, Viognier, Carignan, (Counoise, *Muscardin, Vaccarèse,* Pinot Blanc, Mauzac, *Pascal Blanc,* Ugni Blanc, Camarèse, *Calitor,* Gamay)

Côtes du Rhône Villages RHÔNE Carignan, Grenache, *Camarèse,* Cinsaut, (Clairette, Roussanne, Bourboulenc, Viognier, Picpou Blancl, Marsanne, Grenache Blanc, *Picardin,* Mauzac)

Côtes du Roussillon LANGUEDOC-ROUSSILLON, FRA Syrah, Mourvèdre, Carignan, Macabéo, (Cinsaut, Grenache, Lladoner Pelut)

Côtes de St.-Mont SOUTHWEST, FRA Tannat, (Cabernet Sauvignon, Cabernet Franc, Merlot, Fer)

Côtes de Toul LORRAINE, FRA Pinot Noir, Pinot Meunier, Gamay, (Aligoté, Auxerrois, *Aubin*)

Côtes du Ventoux RHÔNE Grenache, Cinsaut, Mourvèdre, (Carignan, *Picpoul Noir*, Counoise, Clairette, Bourboulenc, Grenache Blanc, Roussanne)

Côtes du Vivarais RHÔNE, FRA Grenache, Syrah, Cinsaut

Côtes Roannaises LOIRE, FRA Gamay

Dão PORTUGAL Alfrocheiro, *Alvarelhão, Aragonez, Bastardo, Jaén, Rufete,* Tinto Cão, Touriga Nacional, Trincadeira

Donnici CALABRIA, ITA Gaglioppo 50% min, *Greco Nero* 10% min, Malvasia, *Pecorello* and/or Greco 20% max, (other local white varieties 10% max, other local red varieties 20% max)

Elba TUSCANY, ITA Sangiovese 75%, other local varieties 25% max

Eloro SICILY, ITA Nero d'Avola, *Pignatello* and/or Frappato 90% (other local red varieties 10% max)

Etna SICILY, ITA Nerello Mascalese 80% min, (Nerello Mantellato 20% max, other local non-aromatic red varieties 10% max)

Faugères LANGUEDOC-ROUSSILLON, FRA Carignan, Cinsaut, Syrah, Mourvèdre, Grenache, Lladoner Pelut

Fiefs Vendéens LOIRE, FRA Gamay, Pinot Noir, Cabernet Sauvignon, Cabernet Franc, Négrette, (*Gamay de Chaudenay*)

Friuli Annia FRIULI-VENEZIA GIULIA, ITA One or more local red varieties as a blend

ROSÉ WINES

Friuli Aquileia FRIULI-VENEZIA GIULIA, ITA Merlot

Friuli Grave FRIULI-VENEZIA GIULIA, ITA One or more local non-aromatic red varieties as a blend

Friuli Latisana FRIULI-VENEZIA GIULIA, Merlot 70-80% (Cabernet Franc, Cabernet sauvignon and/or Refosco 30% max)

Gaillac SOUTHWEST, FRA *Duras, Fer, Syrah, (Gamay, Cabernet Sauvignon, Cabernet Franc, Merlot)*

Galantina APULIA , ITA Negroamaro 65% min, other non-aromatic local red varieties 35% max

Gallucio CAMPANIA, ITA Aglianico 70% min, other local red varieties up to 30%

Garda LOMBARDY & VENETO, ITA *Groppello* 30% max, (Marzemino 5% max, Sangiovese 5% min, Barbera 5% min other local non-aromatic varieties 10% max)

Garda Colli Mantovani LOMBARDY, ITA Merlot 45% max, Rondinella 40% max, (Cabernet 20% max, Sangiovese, Molinara and/or Negrara Trentina 15% max)

Gigondas RHÔNE, FRA Grenache 60%-75%, (*Terret Noir, Picardin, Picpoul Noir,* Roussanne, Marsanne, Bourbolenc, Viogner, *Pascal Blanc,* Mauzac, Pinot Blanc, Camarése, Counoise, *Muscardin, Vaccarèse, Calitor,* Gamay, Cinsaut)

Gioia del Colle APULIA , ITA Primitivo 50-60%, Montepulciano, Sangiovese, Negroamaro and/or Malvasia Nera 40-50%

Golfo del Tigullio LIGURIA, ITA *Ciliegiolo* 20-70%, Dolcetto 20-70%, other local non-aromatic red varieties 40% max

Guardia Sanframondi CAMPANIA, ITA Sangiovese 80%, (other local red varieties 20% max)

Guardiolo CAMPANIA, ITA Sangiovese 80%, (other local red varieties 20% max)

Haut-Poitou LOIRE, FRA Pinot Noir, Cabernet Franc, Cabernet Sauvignon, Gamay, Merlot, Malbec, (Grolleau, *Gamay de Chaudenay*)

Irouléguy SOUTHWEST, FRA Tannat, Cabernet Sauvignon, Cabernet Franc

Jumilla SPAIN Monastrell, (Garnacha Tintorera, Tempranillo, Garnacha, Cabernet Sauvignon)

Jumilla-Monastrell SPAIN Monastrell 85% min, (Garnacha Tintorera, Tempranillo, Garnacha, Cabernet Sauvignon)

L'Oeil-de-Perdrix de Neuchâtel SWITZERLAND Pinot Noir

La Palma SPAIN *Negramoll, (Listán Negro, Malvasía Rosada, Moscatel Negro, Tintilla)*

Lacryma Christi del Vesuvio CAMPANIA, ITA Piedirosso and/or *Sciascinoso* 80%, (Aglianico 20% max)

Lamezia CALABRIA, ITA Nerello Mascalese and/or *Nerello Cappuccio* 30-50%, Gaglioppo and/or *Magliocco* 25-35%, *Greco Nero* and/or *Marsigliana* 25-35%, (other local red varieties 20% max)

Lanzarote SPAIN *Listán Negra, Negramoll*

Les Baux de Provence PROVENCE, FRA Grenache, Mourvèdre, Syrah, (Counoise, Carignan, Cinsaut, Cabernet Sauvignon)

Leverano APULIA, ITA Negroamaro 50% min; Montepulciano, Sangiovese, and/or *Malvasia Nera* 40% max; other local red varieties, 30% max

Lirac RHÔNE, FRA Grenache 40% min, Syrah, Mourvèdre, Cinsaut, (Carignan, Picpoul Blanc, Roussanne, Marsanne, Bourbolenc, Viogner, Ugni Blanc, Grenache Blanc, Clairette)

Lison-Pramaggiore VENETO/FRIULI-VENEZIA GIULIA, ITA Merlot 50-70%, other local non-aromatic red varieties 50% max. The following varietal wines are also made: Cabernet Franc, Cabernet Sauvignon, Malbec, Merlot, Refosco

Lizzano APULIA, ITA Negroamaro 60-80%, Montepulciano, Sangiovese, *Bombino Nero* and/or Pinot Nero 40% max, (other local red varieties 10% max)

Mâcon or Mâcon followed by village name (ie Mâcon-Burgy, Mâcon-Chardonnay, etc) BURGUNDY, FRA Gamay, Pinot Noir, Pinot Gris

Mâcon Supérieur BURGUNDY, FRA Gamay, Pinot Noir, Pinot Gris

Mandrolisai SARDINIA, ITA *Bovale Sardo* 35% min, Grenache, 20-35%, Monica, 20-35%, (other local red varieties 10% max)

Marcillac SOUTHWEST, FRA Fer, Cabernet Franc, Cabernet Sauvignon

Marsannay BURGUNDY, FRA Pinot Noir, Pinot Gris

Matino APULIA, ITA Negroamaro 65% min, Sangiovese and/or Malvasia Nera 35% max

Menetou-Salon BURGUNDY, FRA Pinot Noir

Méntrida SPAIN Garnacha, (*Tinto Basto*, Tempranillo, Cabernet Sauvignon)

Minervois LANGUEDOC-ROUSSILLON, FRA Carignan, Grenache, Lladoner Pelut, Mourvèdre, Syrah, (Cinsaut, *Aspiran Noir, Terret Noir, Picpoul Noir*)

Monferrato PIEDMONT, ITA Barbera, Bonarda Piemontese, Cabernet Franc, Cabernet Sauvignon, Dolcetto, Freisa, Grignolino, Pinot Nero and/or Nebbiolo 85% (other local non-aromatic varieties 15% max)

Montepulciano d'Abruzzo Cerasuolo ABRUZZI, ITA Montepulciano 85% (other local red varieties 15% max)

Monteregio di Massa Marittima TUSCANY, ITA Sangiovese 80% min (other local red varieties 20% max)

Nardò APULIA, ITA Negroamaro 80% min (Montepulciano and/or Malvasia Nera 20% max)

Navarra SPAIN Garnacha, Tempranillo, Merlot, Cabernet Sauvignon, Graciano, Mazuelo

Oltrepo Pavese LOMBARDY, ITA Barbera 25-65%, *Croatina* 25-65%, *Uva Rara, Ughetta* and/or Pinot Nero 45% max. The following varietal wine is also made: Pinot Nero

Orta Nova APULIA, ITA Sangiovese 60%, Uva di Troia, and/or Montepulciano 30-40%, (Lambrusco Maestri and/or Trebbiano Toscano 10% max)

Palette PROVENCE, FRA Grenache, Cinsaut, Mourvèdre, (*Téoulier, Durif,* Syrah, Carignan, Cabernet Sauvignon, Muscat, *Castets, Brun-Fourcat, Terret Gris, Petit-Brun, Tibouren,* Clairette, *Picardan,* Ugni Blanc, *Ugni Rosé,* Grenache Blanc, Picpoul Blanc, *Pascal, Aragnan,* Colombard, *Terret-Bourret*)

Palmela PORTUGAL Castelão, Alfrocheiro, Arinto, *Bastardo,* Cabernet Sauvignon, *Fernão Pires, Moscatel Galego Branco, Moscatel Graúdo, Moscatel Galego Roxo, Rabo de Ovelha, Síria, Tamarez,* Trincadeira, *Vital*

Parrina TUSCANY, ITA Sangiovese 70% min, other local red varieties 30% max

Patrimonio CORSICA, FRA *Nielluccio* 90% min, (Grenache, *Sciacarello,* Vermentino)

Penedés SPAIN Garnacha, Cariñena, Tempranillo, Samsó, Monastrell, Cabernet Sauvignon (Cabernet Franc, Merlot, Pinot Noir)

Pentro di Isernia MOLISE, ITA Montepulciano 45-55%, Sangiovese 45-55%, other local red varieties 10% max

Pic-St.-Loup, Coteaux du Languedoc LANGUEDOC-ROUSSILLON, FRA Grenache, Mourvèdre, Syrah, Carignan

Pinerolese PIEDMONT, ITA Barbera, Bonarda, Nebbiolo and/or *Neretto* 50% min, other local non-aromatic red varieties 50% max

Priorato SPAIN Garnacha Tinta, Garnacha Peluda, Mazuelo, Cariñena, Cabernet Sauvignon

Reuilly LOIRE, FRA Pinot Gris

Ribatejo PORTUGAL Aragonez, Baga, *Camarate*, Castelão, *Preto Martinho*, *Tinta Miúda*, Touriga Franca, Touriga Nacional and/or Trincadeira 50% min, Alfrocheiro, Alicante Bouchet, *Bastardo*, Cabernet Sauvignon, *Caladoc*, *Esgana Cão Tinto*, *Grand Noir, Jaén*, Merlot, *Moreto*, Petit Verdot, Pinot Noir, Tinta Barroca, *Tinta Caiada* and/or Tinto Cão 50% max

Ribera del Guadiana SPAIN Garnacha, Tempranillo, Bobal, Cabernet Sauvignon, Graciano, Mazuelo, Merlot, Monastrell, Syrah

Rioja SPAIN Tempranillo, Garnacha, (Graciano, Mazuelo, Viura)

Riviera del Garda Bresciano LOMBARDY, ITA Barbera 25-65%, *Croatina* 25-65%, *Uva Rara, Ughetta* and/or Pinot Nero 45% max

Rosé de Loire LOIRE, FRA Cabernet Franc, Cabernet Sauvignon, Pinot Noir, Gamay, Pineau d'Aunis, Grolleau

Rosé de Riceys CHAMPAGNE, FRA Pinot Noir

St.-Chinian LANGUEDOC-ROUSSILLON, FRA Carignan, Cinsaut, Grenache, Mourvèdre, Syrah, Lladoner Pelut

St.-Nicolas-de-Bourgueil LOIRE, FRA Cabernet Franc 90-100%, (Cabernet Sauvignon)

Saint-Pourçain LOIRE, FRA Gamay, Pinot Noir, (*Gamay Teinturier*)

Salice Salentino APULIA, ITA Negroamaro 80% min, (Malvasia Nera)

Sancerre LOIRE, FRA Pinot Noir

San Severo APULIA, ITA Montepulciano 70% min, (Sangiovese)

Sant'Agata dei Goti CALABRIA, ITA Aglianico 40-60%, Piedirosso 40-60%, (other local red varieties 20% max)

Sant'Anna di Isola Capo Rizzuto CALABRIA, ITA Gaglioppo 40-60%, *Nocera*, Nerello Mascalese, *Nerello Cappuccio*, Malvasia Nera, Malvasia and/or Greco 40-60%, with the white grape varieties limited to 35%

San Vito di Luzzi CALABRIA, ITA Gaglioppo 70% min, *Greco Nero*, Sangiovese and/or other local red varieties 30% max, (Malvasia 10% max)

Savuto CALABRIA, ITA Gaglioppo 35-45%, *Greco Nero, Nerello Cappuccio, Magliocco Ganino* and/or Sangiovese 30-40%, Malvasia and/or *Pecorino* 25% max

Scavigna CALABRIA, ITA Gaglioppo 60% max, *Nerello Cappuccio* 40% max, other local red varieties 40% max

Sciacca SICILY, ITA Merlot, Cabernet Sauvignon, Nero d'Avola and/or Sangiovese 70%, other local non-aromatic red varieties 30% max

Solopaca CALABRIA, ITA Sangiovese 50-60%, Aglianico 20-40%, Piedirosso, *Sciascinoso* and/or other local red varieties 30% max

Somontano SPAIN *Moristel,* Tempranillo, Garnacha, *Parreleta,* Cabernet Sauvignon

Sovana CALABRIA, ITA Sangiovese 50%, other local non-aromatic red varieties 50% max.

Squinzano APULIA, ITA Negroamaro 70% min, Sangiovese and/or Malvasia Nera 30% max

Tacoronte-Acentejo SPAIN *Listán Negro, Negramol*

Tarquinia LATIUM, ITA Sangiovese and/or Montepulciano 60%, *Cesanese Comune* 25% max, other local red varieties 30% max

Tarragona SPAIN Mazuelo, Garnacha, Tempranillo

Tavel RHÔNE, FRA Grenache, Cinsaut, Clairette, *Picpoul Noir,* Bourboulenc, Mourvèdre, Syrah, (Carignan)

Távora-Varosa PORTUGAL *Alvarelhão,* Aragonez, *Bastardo,* Castelão, Malvasia Preta, *Marufo, Rufete,* Tinta Barroca, *Barca,* Touriga Franca, Touriga Nacional, *Vinhão*

Teroldego Rotaliano TRENTINO-ALTO ADIGE, ITA Teroldego 100%

Terra Alta SPAIN Mazuelo, Garnacha, Garnacha Peluda, Cabernet Sauvignon, Merlot, Tempranillo

Torgiano UMBRIA, ITA, Sangiovese 50-70%, Canaiolo 15-30%, (Trebbiano Toscano 10% max, other local red varieties 15% max)

Touraine LOIRE, FRA Gamay, Cabernet Franc, Grolleau, Pineau d'Aunis, (*Gamay Teninturier, Gamay de Bouze*)

Touraine-Amboise LOIRE, FRA Gamay, Cabernet Franc, Cabernet Sauvignon, Malbec

Touraine Azay-le-Rideau LOIRE, FRA Gamay, Malbec

Touraine-Mesland LOIRE, FRA Cabernet Franc, Cabernet Sauvignon, Malbec, Gamay

Trentino TRENTINO-ALTO ADIGE, ITA *Enantio,* Schiava, Teroldego and/or Lagrein, at least two of each, with 70% max of any one. The following varietal wines are also made: Lagrein, *Moscato Rosa*

Tursan SOUTHWEST, FRA Tannat, Cabernet Franc, Cabernet Sauvignon, Fer

Utiel-Requena SPAIN Bobal, Garnacha, Tempranillo, (Cabernet Sauvignon, Merlot)

Vacqueyras RHÔNE, FRA Grenache (Syrah, Mourvèdre, Cinsaut, *Terret Noir,* Counoise, *Muscardin, Vacarèse,* Gamay, *Camarèse*)

Val di Cornia TUSCANY, ITA Sangiovese 50% min, Cabernet Sauvignon and/or Merlot 50% max (other local red varieties 20% max)

Val Polcevera LIGURIA, ITA Dolcetto, Sangiovese and/or *Ciliegiolo* 60% min, Barbera 40% max

Valdadige VENETO & TRENTINO-ALTO ADIGE, ITA *Enantio* and/or Schiava 50-100%, Merlot, Pinot Nero, Lagrein, Teroldego, Cabernet Franc and/or Cabernet Sauvignon 50% max. The following varietal wine is also made: Schiava

Valdeorras SPAIN Mencía, Garnacha Tintorera, *Gran Negro, María Ardoña*

Valdepeñas SPAIN Tempranillo (Garnacha, Cabernet Sauvignon, Merlot, Pinot Noir, Airén, Macabeo)

Valdichiana TUSCANY, ITA Sangiovese 50%, Cabernet Sauvignon, Cabernet Franc, Merlot and/or Syrah 50% max, (other local non-aromatic red varieties 15% max)

Valençay LOIRE, FRA Cabernet Franc, Cabernet Sauvignon, Malbec, Gamay, (Pineau d'Aunis, *Gamay Teinturier*)

Valencia SPAIN Garnacha, Monsatrell, Tempranillo, *Tintorera, Forcayat*

Valle d'Aosta AOSTA, ITA One or more local red varieties

Valle de la Orotava SPAIN *Listán Negro,* (*Negramoll*)

Verbicaro CALABRIA, ITA Gaglioppo and/or *Greco Nero* 60-80%, Malvasia, *Guarnaccia Bianca* and/or Greco 20-40%, (other local non-aromatic red varieties 20% max)

Vesuvio CAMPANIA, ITA Piedirosso and/or *Sciascinoso* 80%, (Aglianico 20% max)

Vicenza VENETO, ITA Merlot 50%, other local non-aromatic red varieties 50% max. The following varietal wines are also made: Cabernet Sauvignon, Merlot, Pinot Nero, *Raboso*

Vignanello LATIUM, ITA Sangiovese 40-60%, *Ciliegiolo* 40-50% (other local red varieties 20% max)

Vin du Bugey SAVOIE, FRA Gamay, Pinot Noir, *Poulsard, Mondeuse,* (Chardonnay, *Roussette,* Aligoté, *Mondeuse Blanche, Jacquère,* Pinot Gris, *Molette* 20% max)

Vin de Corse CORSICA, FRA *Nielluccio,* Grenache, *Sciacarello,* (Cinsaut, Mourvèdre, *Barbarossa,* Syrah, Carginan, Vermentino)

Vin du Savoie SAVOIE, FRA Gamay, *Mondeuse,* Pinot Noir, (*Persan,* Cabernet Franc, Cabernet Sauvignon, *Etraire de la Dui, Serène, Joubertin,* Chardonnay, *Roussette,* Aligoté, *Mondeuse Blanc, Jacquère,* Pinot Gris, *Gringet, Verdesse,* Chasselas)

Vinho Verde PORTUGAL Amaral, Borraçal, Alvarelhão, Espadeiro, Padeiro, Pedral, Rabo de Anho, Vinhão

Vinos de Madrid SPAIN Tempranillo, Garnacha

Vins d'Entraygues et du Fel SOUTHWEST, FRA Cabernet Franc, Cabernet Sauvignon, Fer, Gamay, *Jurançon Noir,* Merlot, *Mouyssaguès,* Négrette, Pinot Noir

Vins d'Estaing SOUTHWEST, FRA Fer, Gamay, *Abouriou, Jurançon Noir,* Merlot, Cabernet Franc, Cabernet Sauvignon, *Mouyssaguès,* Négrette, Pinot Noir, *Duras, Castet*

Vins de l'Orléanais LOIRE, FRA Pinot Noir, Pinot Meunier, Cabernet Franc

Vins du Thouarsais LOIRE, FRA Cabernet Franc, Cabernet Sauvignon, Gamay

White Zinfandel USA Zinfandel

Ycoden-Daute-Isora SPAIN *Listán Negro,* (*Bastardo Negra, Malvasía Rosada, Moscatel Negro, Negramoll, Tintilla, Vijariego Negra*)

Yecla SPAIN Monastrell, Garnacha, (Tempranillo, Cabernet Sauvignon, Merlot, Syrah)

ROSÉ WINES

SPARKLING WINES

Acqui PIEDMONT, ITA Brachetto

Aglianico del Vulture BASILICATA, ITA Aglianico

Alcamo SICILY, ITA **white:** Catarratto 80% min, (*Grecanico*, Inzolia, *Grillo*, Chardonnay, Müller Thurgau and/or Sauvignon Blanc 20% max), **rosé:** Nerello Mascalese, Nero d'Avola, Sangiovese, Frappato, *Perricone*, Cabernet Sauvignon, Merlot and/or Syrah, **red:** Nero d'Avola 60% min, Sangiovese, Frappato, *Perricone*, Cabernet Sauvignon, Merlot and/or Syrah 40% max, (other local varieties 10% max)

Alta Langa PIEDMONT, ITA **white, rosé, and red:** Pinot Nero and/or Chardonnay 90-100%, (other local non-aromatic varieties 10% max)

Anjou Mousseux LOIRE, FRA **white:** Chenin Blanc 60% min, (Cabernet Sauvignon, Cabernet Franc, Malbec, Gamay, Grolleau, Pineau d'Aunis), **rosé:** Cabernet Sauvignon, Cabernet Franc, Malbec, Grolleau, Pineau d'Aunis

Anjou Pétillant LOIRE, FRA Chenin Blanc 80% min, (Chardonnay, Sauvignon Blanc)

Arbois Mousseux JURA, FRA Savagnin, Chardonnay, Pinot Blanc

Arcole VENETO, ITA Garganega 50% min, (other local non-aromatic white varieties 50% max)

Asti PIEDMONT, ITA Moscato

Asti Spumante PIEDMONT, ITA Moscato

Aversa CAMPANIA, ITA *Asprinio* 85% min, other local white varieties 15% max

Bagnoli (di Sopra) VENETO, ITA **white & rosé:** *Raboso Piave* and/or *Raboso Veronese* 40% min, (Chardonnay 20% min, other local non-aromatic varieties 10% max)

Bairrada Espumante PORTUGAL Arinto, Bical, *Cercial,* Chardonnay, *Fernão Pires, Rabo de Ovelha,* Sauvignon Blanc, *Sercealinho,* Verdelho

Bardolino VENETO, ITA **rosé:** Corvina 35-65%, Rondinella 10-40%, (Molinara 10-20%, *Negrara* 10%, *Rossignola,* Barbera, Sangiovese and/or Garganega 15% max)

Bianco di Custoza VENETO, ITA Trebbiano Toscano 20-45%, Garganega 20-40%, Tocai Friulano 5-30%, Cortese, Riesling Italico, Pinot Blanc, Chardonnay and/or Malvasia Toscana 20-30%

Bianco di Pitigliano TUSCANY, ITA Trebbiano Toscano 50-80% (Greco, Malvasia Bianca Toscana and/or Verdello 20%, Grechetto 15% max, Chardonnay, Sauvignon Blanc, Pinot Bianco and/or Riesling Italico 15% max, other local white varieties 10% max)

Blanquette de Limoux LANGUEDOC-ROUSSILLON, FRA Mauzac 90% min, (Chenin Blanc, Chardonnay)

Blanquette Méthode Ancestrale LANGUEDOC-ROUSSILLON, FRA Mauzac

Bourgogne Mousseux BURGUNDY, FRA **red:** Pinot Noir, Gamay, (*César, Tressot*)

Brachetto d'Acqui PIEDMONT, ITA Brachetto

Bucelas Espumante PORTUGAL Arinto 75% min, Sercial and/or *Rabo de Ovelha* 25% max

Caluso PIEDMONT, ITA Erbaluce

Campi Flegrei CAMPANIA, ITA Falanghina 50-70%, *Biancolella* and/or Coda di Volpe 10-30%, other local white varieties 30% max

Cava SPAIN **white:** Macabeo, Parellada, Xarel-lo, (Chardonnay, Malvasia, Pinot Noir), **rosé:** Macabeo, Parellada, Xarel-lo, (Chardonnay, Garnacha, Malvasia, Pinot Noir, Mourvèdre)

Cesanese del Piglio LATIUM, ITA *Cesanese di Affile* and/or *Cesanese Comune* 90% min, (Sangiovese, Montepulciano, Barbera, Trebbiano Toscano and/or Bombino Bianco 10% max)

Cesanese di Affile LATIUM, ITA *Cesanese di Affile* and/or *Cesanese Comune* 90% min, (Sangiovese, Montepulciano, Barbera, Trebbiano Toscano and/or Bombino Bianco 10% max)

Cesanese di Olevano Romano LATIUM, ITA *Cesanese di Affile* and/or *Cesanese Comune* 90% min, (Sangiovese, Montepulciano, Barbera, Trebbiano Toscano and/or Bombino Bianco 10% max)

Champagne CHAMPAGNE, FRA Pinot Noir, Pinot Meunier, Chardonnay

> **Dom Perignon**, a famous Champagne, is typically 60% Chardonnay and 40% Pinot Noir
>
> **Krug**, another famous Champagne, is typically 32% Chardonnay, 46% Pinot Noir and 22% Pinot Meunier.

Champagne Blanc de Blancs CHAMPAGNE, FRA Chardonnay

Champagne Blanc de Noirs CHAMPAGNE, FRA Pinot Noir, Pinot Meunier

Clairette de Die Méthode Dioise Ancestrale RHÔNE, FRA Muscat Blanc 75-100%, (Clairette)

Colli Albani LATIUM, ITA Malvasia di Candia 60% max, Trebbiano Toscano, Trebbiano Romagnolo, Trebbiano Giallo and/or Trebbiano di Soave 25-50%, Malvasia del Lazio 5-45%, (other local white varieties 10% max)

Colli Berici VENETO, ITA Garganega 50% min, Pinot Bianco, Pinot Grigio, Chardonnay and/or Sauvignon Blanc 50% max

Colli Bolognesi EMILIA-ROMAGNA, ITA The following varietal wines are also made: Chardonnay, *Pignoletto*, Pinot Bianco, Riesling Italico

Colli del Trasimeno UMBRIA, ITA Chardonnay, Pinot Blanc, Pinot Grigio, Pinot Nero and/or Grechetto 70%, other local white varieties 30% max

Colli di Parma EMILIA-ROMAGNA, ITA Pinot Nero, Pinot Bianco and/or Chardonnay

Colli di Scandiano e Canossa EMILIA-ROMAGNA, ITA Sauvignon Blanc 40-80%, Malvasia, Trebbiano, Pinot Bianco and/or Pinot Grigio 20-60%

Colli Maceratesi MARCHES, ITA *Maceratino* 70%, Trebbiano Toscano, Verdicchio, Malvasia Toscana, Chardonnay, Sauvignon Blanc, *Incrocio Bruni 54*, *Pecorino* and/or Grechetto 30% max (other local white varieties 15% max)

Colli Perugini UMBRIA, ITA Grechetto, Chardonnay, Pinot Bianco, Pinot Nero and/or Pinot Grigio 80% min (other local white varieties 20% max)

Colli Piacentini EMILIA-ROMAGNA, ITA The following varietal wines are also made: Bonarda, Chardonnay, Malvasia, *Ortugo*, Pinot Grigio, Pinot Nero

Colli Piacentini Trebbianino Val Trebbia EMILIA-ROMAGNA, ITA
Ortrugo 35-65%, Malvasia and/or Moscato Bianco 10-20%, Trebbiano
and/or Sauvignon Blanc 15-30%, (other local white varieties 15%
max)

Colli Piacentini Valnure EMILIA-ROMAGNA, ITA Malvasia 20-50%,
Ortrugo and/or Trebbiano 20-65%, (other local white varieties 15%
max)

Colli Tortonesi PIEDMONT, ITA Cortese

Contea di Sclafani SICILY, ITA **white:** Catarratto, Inzolia and/or
Grecanico 50%, other local white varieties 50% max. The following
varietal wines are also made: Catarratto, Chardonnay, *Grecanico*, *Grillo*,
Inzolia, Pinot Bianco, Sauvignon Blanc, **rosé:** Nerello Mascalese 50%,
other local red varieties 50% max

Controguerra ABRUZZO, ITA Trebbiano 60% min, Verdicchio and/or
Pecorino 30% min, (other local white varieties 10% max)

Cortese dell'Alto Monferrato PIEDMONT, ITA Cortese 85%, (other local
white varieties 15% max)

Coteaux Champenois CHAMPAGNE, FRA Pinot Noir, Pinot Meunier,
Chardonnay

Côtes du Jura Mousseux JURA, FRA Savagnin, Chardonnay, Pinot Blanc

Crémant d'Alsace ALSACE, FRA Pinot Blanc, Pinot Gris, Auxerrois,
Chardonnay, Riesling

Crémant de Bordeaux BORDEAUX, FRA **red:** Cabernet Sauvignon,
Cabernet Franc, Merlot, (Malbec, Petit Verdot, Carmenère, Ugni
Blanc, Colombard), **white:** Sémillon, Sauvignon Blanc, Muscadelle,
(Colombard, Ugni Blanc), **rosé:** Cabernet Sauvignon, Cabernet Franc,
Merlot, (Malbec, Petit Verdot, Carmenère)

Crémant de Bourgogne BURGUNDY, FRA **white & rosé:** Pinot noir,
Pinot Gris, Pinot Blanc, Chardonnay, Aligoté, Melon de Bourgogne,
Sacy, (Gamay)

Crémant de Die RHÔNE, FRA Clairette

Crémant du Jura JURA, FRA Savagnin, Chardonnay, Pinot Blanc

Crémant de Limoux LANGUEDOC-ROUSSILLON, FRA Mauzac 60-70%,
(Chenin Blanc, Chardonnay)

Crémant de Loire LOIRE, FRA **white:** Chenin Blanc, (Chardonnay,
Sauvignon Blanc, Cabernet Sauvignon, Cabernet Franc, *Arbois*, Pinot
d'Aunis, Pinot Noir), **rosé:** Cabernet Franc, Grolleau, (Cabernet
Sauvignon, Pinot d'Aunis, Pinot Noir, *Arbois*, Chardonnay)

Dão Espumante PORTUGAL *Barcelo*, Bical, *Cercial, Encruzado*, Malvasia
Fina, *Rabo de Ovelha, Terrantez, Uva Cão*, Verdelho

Delia Nivolelli SICILY, ITA *Grecanico*, Chardonnay and/or Inzolia,
Damaschino and/or *Grillo* 100%. The following varietal wines are also
made: Chardonnay, *Damaschino, Grecanico, Grillo*, Inzolia

Est! Est!! Est!!! di Montefiascone LATIUM, ITA Trebbiano Toscano
65%, (Malvasia Toscana 20% max, Trebbiano Giallo 15% max)

Franciacorta LOMBARDY, ITA **white:** Chardonnay, Pinot Bianco and/or
Pinot Nero, **rosé:** Chardonnay and/or Pinot Bianco max 85%, (Pinot
Nero min 15%)

Frascati LATIUM, ITA Malvasia di Candia and/or Trebbiano Toscano 70%
min, Greco and/or Malvasia del Lazio 30% max, (other local white
varieties 10% max)

Freisa d'Asti PIEDMONT, ITA Fresia

Freisa di Chieri PIEDMONT, ITA Fresia

Friuli Latisana FRIULI-VENEZIA GIULIA Chardonnay, Pinot Bianco and/ or Pinot Nero 90% (other local white varieties 10% max.)

Gaillac Mousseux SOUTHWEST, FRA **white:** Len de l'EL, Sauvignon Blanc, Mauzac, *Mauzac Rose,* Muscadelle, *Ondenc,* Sémillion, **rosé:** *Duras,* (Fer, Syrah, Gamay, Cabernet Sauvignon, Cabernet Franc, Merlot)

Golfo del Tigullio LIGURIA, ITA Vermentino 20-70%, *Bianchetta Genovese* 20-70%, other local non-aromatic white varieties 40% max

Gravina APULIA , ITA Malvasia, Greco, *Bianco d'Alessano,* (Bombino Bianco, Trebbiano, *Verdeca)*

Guardia Sanframondi CAMPANIA, ITA Falanghina 70%, other local white varieties 30% max

Guardiolo CAMPANIA, ITA Falanghina 70%, other local white varieties 30% max

Lacryma Christi del Vesuvio CAMPANIA, ITA Coda di Volpe and/or *Verdeca* 80% (Falanghina and/or Greco 20% max)

L'Étoile Mousseux JURA, FRA Savagnin, *Poulsard,* Chardonnay

Lizzano APULIA, ITA **white:** Trebbiano 40-60%, Chardonnay and/or Pinot Bianco 30% min, (Malvasia, Sauvignon Blanc, *Bianco di Alessano),* **rosé:** Negroamaro 60-80%, Montepulciano, Sangiovese, *Bombino Nero* and/or Pinot Nero 40% max, (other local red varieties 10% max)

Locorotondo APULIA, ITA *Verdeca* 50-65%, *Bianco d'Alessano* 35-50%, (Fiano, Bombino Bianco, Malvasia 5% max)

Lugana LOMBARDY/VENETO, ITA Trebbiano di Lugana 90% min (other local non-aromatic white varieties 10% max)

Malvasia di Casorzo d'Asti PIEDMONT, ITA Malvasia Nera di Casorzo 90%, (Freisa, Grignolino, Barbera and/or other local aromatic varieties 10% max)

Malvasia di Castelnuovo Don Bosco PIEDMONT, ITA Malvasia di Schierano 85%, (Freisa 15% max)

Marino LATIUM, ITA Malvasia di Candia 60% max, Trebbiano Toscano, Trebbiano Romagnolo, Trebbiano Giallo and/or Trebbiano di Soave 25-55%, Malvasia del Lazio 5-45%, (other local non-aromatic white varieties 10% max)

Martina / Martina Franca APULIA, ITA *Verdeca* 50-65%, *Bianco d'Alessano* 35-50%, (Fiano, Bombino Bianco, Malvasia 5% max)

Molise MOLISE, ITA Chardonnay, Pinot Bianco and/or Moscato 50% min, other local white varieties 50% max

Montello e Colli Asolani Prosecco VENETO, ITA Prosecco 85% min (*Bianchetta Trevigiana*, Chardonnay, Pinot Bianco, Pinot Grigio and/or Riesling Italico 15% max)

Monti Lessini Durello Spumante VENETO, ITA *Durello* 85%, Garganega and/or Trebbiano di Soave, Pinot Bianco, Pinot Nero and/or Chardonnay 15%

Monti Lessini Spumante VENETO, ITA Chardonnay 50% min, Pinot Bianco and/or Pinot Nero 50% max

Montlouis Mousseux LOIRE, FRA Chenin Blanc

Montlouis Pétillant LOIRE, FRA Chenin Blanc

Moscadello di Montalcino TUSCANY, ITA Moscato 85% min (other local white varieties 15% max)

Moscato d'Asti PIEDMONT, ITA Moscato

Moscato di Cagliari SARDINIA, ITA Moscato

Moscato di Noto SICILY, ITA Moscato

Moscato di Pantelleria SICILY, ITA Zibbibo

Moscato di Sardegna SARDINIA, ITA Moscato 90% (other local white varieties 10% max)

Nebbiolo d'Alba PIEDMONT, ITA Nebbiolo

Offida Passerina MARCHES, ITA *Passerina* 85% (other local non-aromatic white varieties 15% max)

Oltrepo Pavese Spumante LOMBARDY, ITA Pinot Nero 70%, Chardonnay, Pinot Grigio and/or Pinot Bianco 30% max. The following varietal wines are also made: Chardonnay, Cortese, Malvasia, Moscato, Riesling Italico, Sauvignon Blanc

Palmela Espumante PORTUGAL Castelão, Alfrocheiro, Arinto, *Bastardo*, Cabernet Sauvignon, *Fernão Pires*, *Moscatel Galego Branco*, *Moscatel Graúdo*, *Moscatel Galego Roxo*, *Rabo de Ovelha*, *Síria*, *Tamarez*, Trincadeira, *Vital*

Piemonte Spumante PIEDMONT, ITA Chardonnay, Pinot Bianco, Pinot Grigio and/or Pinot Nero 100%. The following varietal wines are also made: Brachetto, Chardonnay, Cortese, Chardonnay-Pinot, Pinot Bianco, Pinot Grigio, Pinot Nero

Planalto Mirandês Espumante PORTUGAL **red:** *Alvarelhão*, Aragonez, Pinot Noir, *Barca*, Tinta Barroca, Touriga Franca, Touriga Nacional **white:** Bical, Arinto, Chardonnay, *Dona Branca*, *Fernão Pires*, *Folgasão*, Gouveio, Malvasia Fina, Malvasia Rei, Pinot Blanc

Prosecco di Conegliano-Valdobbiadene VENETO, ITA Prosecco 85%, (*Verdisio*, *Bianchetta*, *Perera* and/or *Prosecco Lungo* 15% max)

Recioto di Soave VENETO, ITA Garganega 70% min, (Pinot Bianco, Chardonnay, Trebbiano)

Romagna Albana Spumante EMILIA-ROMAGNA, ITA Albana

Rueda Espumoso SPAIN Verdejo 85% min, (Sauvignon Blanc, Macabeo and/or Palomino 15% max)

St.-Péray RHÔNE, FRA Marsanne, Roussanne

Salice Salentino PUGLIA, ITA **white:** Pinot Bianco 85% (Chardonnay and/or Sauvignon Blanc 15% max, **rosé:** Negroamaro 80% min, (Malvasia Nera 20% max)

Sannio CAMPANIA, ITA Aglianico, Greco and/or Falanghina

Sardegna Semidano Spumante SARDINIA, ITA *Semidano* 85% (other local white varieties 15% max)

Saumur Mousseux LOIRE, FRA **white:** Chenin Blanc, (Chardonnay, Sauvignon Blanc, Cabernet Sauvignon, Cabernet Franc, Malbec, Gamay, Grolleau, Pinot d'Aunis, Pinot Noir), **rosé:** Cabernet Franc, Cabernet Sauvignon, (Malbec, Gamay, Grolleau, Pinot d'Aunis, Pinot Noir)

Saumur Pétillant LOIRE, FRA Chenin Blanc 80% min, (Chardonnay, Sauvignon Blanc)

Seyssel Mousseux SAVOIE, FRA Chasselas, *Roussette*

Soave Spumante VENETO, ITA Garganega 70-100%, Pinot Bianco, Chardonnay and/or Trebbiano di Soave 30% max (other local non-aromatic white varieties 5% max)

Solopaca Spumante CAMPANIA, ITA Falanghina 60-100%, other local non-aromatic white varieties 40% max

Taburno Spumante CAMPANIA, ITA Coda di Volpe and/or Falanghina 60%, other local white varieties 40% max

Torgiano Spumante UMBRIA, ITA Chardonnay 40-50%, Pinot Nero 40-50% (other local white varieties 15% max)

Touraine Mousseux LOIRE, FRA **red:** Cabernet Franc, **white:** Chenin Blanc, Sauvignon Blanc (*Arbois*, Chardonnay),

    rosé: Cabernet Franc, Malbec, Gamay, Grolleau

Touraine Pétillant LOIRE, FRA **red:** Cabernet Franc, **white:** Chenin Blanc, (*Arbois*, Chardonnay, Cabernet Franc, Malbec, Grolleau, Pinot d'Aunis, Pinot Noir, Pinot Gris, Pinot Meunier, **rosé:** Cabernet Franc, Malbec, Gamay, Grolleau

Trento Spumante Classico TRENTINO-ALTO ADIGE, ITA **white & rosé:** Chardonnay, Pinot Bianco, Pinot nero and/or Pinot Meunier

Val Polcevera Spumante LIGURIA, ITA Vermentino, *Bianchetta*, *Genovese* and/or *Albarola* 60% min, Pigato, *Rollo* and/or *Bosco* 40% max

Valle d'Aosta Blanc de Morgex et de la Salle AOSTA, ITA *Prié*

Velletri Spumante LATIUM, ITA Malvasia di Candia and/or Malvasia Puntinata 70% max, Trebbiano 30%, (*Bellone*, Bombino Bianco and/or other local white varieties 20% max)

Verdicchio dei Castelli di Iesi Spumante MARCHES, ITA Verdicchio 85% min, (Malvasia Toscana and/or Trebbiano 15% max)

Verdicchio di Matelica Spumante MARCHES, ITA Verdicchio 85% min, (Malvasia Toscana and/or Trebbiano 15% max)

Vernaccia di Serrapetrona Spumante MARCHES, ITA Vernaccia Nera 85%, (other local red varieties 15% max)

Vermentino di Sardegna Spumante SARDINIA, ITA Vermentino 85%, (other local white varieties 15% max)

Vicenza Spumante VENETO, ITA Garganega 50%, other local non-aromatic white varieties 50%. The following varietal wines are also made: Chardonnay, Garganega, Pinot Bianco, Moscato

Vignanello Greco Spumante LATIUM, ITA Greco 85% (other local white varieties 15% max)

Vin du Bugey Cerdon Mousseux SAVOIE, FRA Chardonnay, *Roussette*, Aligoté, *Mondeuse Blanc, Jacquère,* Pinot Gris, *Molette*

Vin du Bugey Cerdon Pétillant SAVOIE, FRA Chardonnay, *Roussette*, Aligoté, *Mondeuse Blanc*, Jacquère, Pinot Gris, *Molette*

Vin du Bugey Pétillant SAVOIE, FRA Chardonnay, *Roussette*, Aligoté, *Mondeuse Blanc*, Jacquère, Pinot Gris, *Molette*

Vin du Savoie Ayze Pétillant SAVOIE, FRA *Roussette, Gringet, (Roussette d'Ayze)*

Vin du Savoie Mousseux SAVOIE, FRA Chardonnay, *Roussette*, Aligoté, *Mondeuse Blanc, Jacquère,* Pinot Gris, (*Molette,* Chasselas, *Gringet,* Roussette d'Ayze, *Verdese*)

Vin du Savoie Pétillant SAVOIE, FRA Aligoté, Chardonnay, *Jacquère*, Roussette, *Mondeuse Blanc,* Malvoisie, (Chasselas, *Gringet, Roussette d'Ayze,* Marsanne, *Verdesse*)

Vouvray Mousseux LOIRE, FRA Chenin Blanc (*Arbois*)

Vouvray Pétillant LOIRE, FRA Chenin Blanc (*Arbois*)

Albana di Romagna EMILIA-ROMAGNA, ITA Albana

Aleatico di Gradoli LATIUM, ITA Aleatico

Aleatico di Puglia PUGLIA,ITA Aleatico 85%, (Negroamaro, Malvasia Nera and/or Primitivo 15% max)

Anjou Coteaux de la Loire LOIRE, FRA Chenin Blanc

Arbois Vin de Paille JURA, FRA *Poulsard, Trousseau*, Savagnin, Chardonnay

Banyuls LANGUEDOC-ROUSSILLON, FRA Grenache 50% min, (Macabeo, Muscat Blanc, Carignan, Cinsaut, Syrah, *Grenache Gris*, Grenache Blanc, *Tourbat*, Muscat d'Alexandria)

Banyuls Grand Cru LANGUEDOC-ROUSSILLON, FRA Grenache 75% min, (Macabeo, Muscat Blanc, Carignan, Cinsaut, Syrah, *Grenache Gris*, Grenache Blanc, *Tourbat*, Muscat d'Alexandrie)

Barsac BORDEAUX, FRA Sémillon, Sauvignon Blanc, Muscadelle

Beaumes-de-Venise, Muscat de RHÔNE, FRA Muscat Blanc

Bianco Capena LATIUM, ITA Malvasia di Candia from Lazio and Toscana 55% min (Trebbiano Toscano, *Romagnolo* and/or *Giallo* 25% min, *Bellone* and Bombino 20% max)

Bianco della Valdinievole TUSCANY, ITA Trebbiano Toscano 70% min, Malvasia del Chianti, *Canaiolo Bianco* and/or Vermentino 25% max, (other local white varieties 5% max)

Bianco dell'Empolese TUSCANY, ITA Trebbiano Toscano 80%, (other local white varieties 20% max)

Bianco di Custoza VENETO, ITA Trebbiano Toscano 20-45%, Garganega 20-40%, Tocai Friulano 5-30%, Cortese, Riesling Italico, Pinot Bianco, Chardonnay and/or Malvasia Toscana 20-30%

Bianco Pisano di San Torpé TUSCANY, ITA Trebbiano Toscano 75%, other local white varieties 25% max

Biscoitos PORTUGAL Verdelho, Arinto, *Terrantez*

Bolgheri Vin Santo Occhio di Pernice TUSCANY, ITA Sangiovese 50-70%, Malvasia Nera 50-70%, other local red varieties 30% max

Bonnezeaux LOIRE, FRA Chenin Blanc

Bordeaux Côtes-de-Francs Liquoreux BORDEAUX, FRA Sémillon, Sauvignon Blanc, Muscadelle

Bordeaux Haut-Benauge BORDEAUX, FRA Sémillon, Sauvignon Blanc, (Muscadelle)

Cadillac BORDEAUX, FRA Sémillon, Sauvignon Blanc, (Muscadelle)

Caluso Passito PIEDMONT, ITA Erbaluce

Candia dei Colli Apuani TUSCANY, ITA Vermentino 70-80% (*Albarola* 10-20%, *Trebbiano* and/or Malvasia del Chianti 20%)

Cannonau di Sardegna SARDINIA, ITA Grenache 90%, (other local red varieties 10% max)

Capalbio TUSCANY, ITA Trebbiano 50% min, other local non-aromatic white varieties 50% max

Carmignano Vin Santo TUSCANY, ITA Trebbiano and/or Malvasia del Chianti 75% min, other local white varieties 25% max

Carmignano Vin Santo Occhio di Pernice TUSCANY, ITA Sangiovese 50% min, other local red or white varieties 50% max

Carcavelos PORTUGAL Castelão, *Preto Martinho*, *Galego Dourado*, *Ratinho* and/or Arinto 75% min, (other local varieties 25% max)

Casteller TRENTINO-ALTO ADIGE, ITA Schiava 30-100%, Lambrusco 60% max, (Merlot, Lagrein and/or Teroldego 20% max)

Castelli Romani LATIUM, ITA *Cesanese*, Merlot, Montepulciano, *Nero Buono* and/or Sangiovese 85% min, (other local red varieties 15% max)

Cérons BORDEAUX, FRA Sémillon, Sauvignon Blanc, (Muscadelle)

Cerveteri LATIUM, ITA **red:** Sangiovese and/or Montepulciano 60%, *Cesanese* 25%, Canaiolo, Carignano and Barbera 30% max, **white:** Trebbiano Toscano, Trebbiano Romagnolo and Trebbiano Giallo 50% min, Malvasia di Candia and Malvasia del Lazo 35% max, (Tocai Friulano, Verdicchio, *Bellone* and/or Bombino Bianco 15% max)

Cesanese del Piglio LATIUM, ITA *Cesanese di Affile* and/or *Cesanese Comune* 90% min, (Sangiovese, Montepulciano, Barbera, Trebbiano Toscano and/or Bombino Bianco 10% max)

Cesanese di Affile LATIUM, ITA *Cesanese di Affile* and/or *Cesanese Comune* 90% min, (Sangiovese, Montepulciano, Barbera, Trebbiano Toscano and/or Bombino Bianco 10% max)

Cesanese di Olevano Romano LATIUM, ITA *Cesanese di Affile* and/or *Cesanese Comune* 90% min, (Sangiovese, Montepulciano, Barbera, Trebbiano Toscano and/or Bombino Bianco 10% max)

Cinque Terre Sciacchetrà LIGURIA, ITA *Bosco* 40% min, (*Albarola* and/or Vermentino 20% max, other local varieties 20% max)

Circeo LATIUM, ITA **red & rosé:** Merlot 85% min, (other local red varieties 15% max), **white:** Trebbiano Toscano 60% min, Malvasia di Candia 30% max, other local white varieties 30% max

Clairette du Languedoc Rancio LANGUEDOC-ROUSSILLON, FRA Clairette

Colli Albani LATIUM, ITA Malvasia di Candia 60% max, Trebbiano Toscano, Trebbiano Romagnolo, Trebbiano Giallo and/or Trebbiano di Soave 25-50%, Malvasia del Lazio 5-45%, (other local white varieties 10% max)

Colli di Rimini Rebola Passito EMILIA-ROMAGNA, ITA *Pignoletto* 85% min, other local white varieties 15% max

Colli Etruschi Viterbesi LATIUM, ITA Moscato

Colli Maceratesi Passito MARCHES, ITA *Maceratino* 70%, Trebbiano Toscano, Verdicchio, Malvasia Toscana, Chardonnay, Sauvignon Blanc, Grechetto, *Incrocio Bruni 54* and/or *Pecorino* 30% max, (other local white varieties 15%)

Colli Perugini Vin Santo UMBRIA, ITA Trebbiano Toscano 50% min, other local white varieties 50% max (Malvasia 10% max)

Colli Piacentini Vin Santo EMILIA-ROMAGNA, ITA Malvasia, *Ortrugo*, Sauvignon Blanc, Marsanne and/or Trebbiano 80%, (other local white varieties 20% max)

Colli Piacentini Vin Santo di Vigoleno EMILIA-ROMAGNA, ITA Marsanne, *Beverdino*, Sauvignon Blanc, *Ortrugo* and/or Trebbiano 60%, other local white varieties 40% max

Colline Saluzzesi PIEDMONT, ITA *Quagliano*

Contea di Sclafani SICILY, ITA Inzolia, Catarratto, *Grecanico, Grillo,* Chardonnay, Pinot Bianco and/or Sauvignon Blanc 100%. The following varietal wines are also made: Catarratto, Chardonnay, *Grecanico, Grillo,* Inzolia, Pinot Bianco, Sauvignon Blanc

Controguerra Passito ABRUZZO, ITA **red:** Montepulciano 60% min, other local red varieties 40% max, **white:** Malvasia and/or *Passerina* 60% min, other local white varieties 40% max

Cori LATIUM, ITA Malvasia di Candia 70% max, Trebbiano Toscano 40% max, *Bellone* and/or Trebbiano Giallo 30% max

Cortona Vin Santo TUSCANY, ITA Sangiovese 85% (other local non-aromatic red varieties 15% max)

Cortona Vin Santo Occhio di Pernice TUSCANY, ITA Sangiovese and/or Malvasia nera 80% (other local non-aromatic red varieties 20% max)

Coteaux de l'Aubance LOIRE, FRA Chenin Blanc

Coteaux du Layon LOIRE, FRA Chenin Blanc

Coteaux du Layon-Chaume LOIRE, FRA Chenin Blanc

Coteaux du Layon Villages LOIRE, FRA Chenin Blanc

Coteaux du Saumur LOIRE, FRA Chenin Blanc

Côtes du Jura Vin de Paille JURA, FRA *Poulsard, Trousseau,* Savagnin, Chardonnay

Cotnari ROMANIA *Grasa, Tamîioasa, Francusa,* Feteasca Alba

Cream Sherry SPAIN Pedro Ximénez, Moscatel (Palomino)

De Licor Moscatel Alicante SPAIN Moscatel

Dolcetto delle Langhe Monregalesi Sciacchettrà PIEDMONT, ITA Dolcetto

Elba Vin Santo TUSCANY, ITA Trebbiano and/or Malvasia Bianca 70%, other local white varieties 30% max

Elba Vin Santo Occhio di Pernice TUSCANY, ITA Sangiovese 50-70%, Malvasia Nera 10-50%, other local red varieties 30% max

Est! Est!! Est!!! di Montefiascone LATIUM, ITA Trebbiano Toscano 65%, (Malvasia Toscana 20% max, Trebbiano Giallo 15% max)

Fondillón de Alicante SPAIN Monastrell

Frascati LATIUM, ITA Malvasia di Candia and/or Trebbiano Toscano 70% min, Greco and/or Malvasia del Lazio 30% max, (other local white varieties 10% max)

Friuli Isonzo Vendemmia Tardiva FRIULI-VENEZIA GIULIA, ITA Tocai Friulano, Sauvignon Blanc, *Verduzzo Friulano,* Pinot Bianco and/or Chardonnay

Gaillac Doux SOUTHWEST, FRA Len de l'El, Sauvignon Blanc, Mauzac, *Mauzac Rose,* Muscadelle, *Ondenc,* Sémillon

Gambellara, Recioto di VENETO, ITA Garganega 80% (other local non-aromatic white varieties 20% max)

Gambellara, Vin Santo di VENETO, ITA Garganega 80% (other local non-aromatic white varieties 20% max)

Golfo del Tigullio Moscato LIGURIA, ITA Moscato

Graves Supérieur BORDEAUX, FRA Sémillon, Sauvignon Blanc, Muscadelle

Gravina APULIA , ITA Malvasia, Greco, *Bianco d'Alessano,* (Bombino Bianco, Trebbiano, *Verdeca*)

Greco di Bianco CALABRIA, ITA Greco 95% min, (other local white varieties)

Haut-Montravel SOUTHWEST, FRA Sauvignon Blanc, Muscadelle, Sémillion

Lanzarote SPAIN Malvasía, (*Breval, Burrablanca, Diego*, Listán, Moscatel, Pedro Ximénez)

Leverano Passito APULIA, ITA Malvasia 50% min, Bombino Bianco 40% max, other local white varieties 30%

Loazzolo PIEDMONT, ITA Moscato

Loupiac BORDEAUX, FRA Sémillon, Sauvignon Blanc, (Muscadelle)

Macvin JURA, FRA **red:** *Poulsard, Trousseau*, Pinot Noir, **white:** *Poulsard,* Savagnin, Chardonnay, **rosé:** *Poulsard, Trousseau*, Pinot Noir

Madeira PORTUGAL Malvasia, Sercial, Verdelho, Bual, Tinta Negra Mole, *Folgasão*

Málaga SPAIN Moscatel, Pedro Ximénez

Malvasia delle Lipari SICILY, ITA Malvasia di Lipari 95% max, (*Corinto Nero* 5%)

Malvasia di Bosa SARDINIA, ITA Malvasia di Bosa

Malvasia di Cagliari SARDINIA, ITA Malvasia di Sardegna

Malvasia di Casorzo d'Asti PIEDMONT, ITA Malvasia Nera di Casorzo 90%, (Freisa, Grignolino, Barbera and/or other local aromatic varieties 10% max)

Malvasia di Castelnuovo Don Bosco PIEDMONT, ITA Malvasia di Schierano 85%, (Freisa 15% max)

Marino LATIUM, ITA Malvasia di Candia 60% max, Trebbiano Toscano, Trebbiano Romagnolo, Trebbiano Giallo and/or Trebbiano di Soave 25-55%, Malvasia del Lazio 5-45%, (other local non-aromatic white varieties 10% max)

Marsala - Oro and Ambra SICILY, ITA *Grillo*, Catarratto, Ansonica and/or *Damaschino*

Marsala - Rubino SICILY, ITA *Perricone*, Calabrese and/or Nerello Mascalese 70%, other local white varieties 30% max

Maury LANGUEDOC-ROUSSILLON, FRA Grenache 75% min, (Macabéo, Muscat Blanc, Carignan, Cinsaut, Syrah, *Grenache Gris*, Grenache Blanc, *Tourbat*, Muscat d'Alexandrie, *Listan*)

Mavrodaphne of Cephalonia / Kefaloniá GREECE Mavrodaphne

Mavrodaphne of Patras / Pátra GREECE Mavrodaphne

Molise Moscato MOLISE, ITA Moscato (other local white varieties 15% max). The following varietal wine is also made: Pinot Bianco

Monbazillac SOUTHWEST, FRA Sémillon, Sauvignon Blanc, Muscadelle

Monica di Cagliari SARDINIA, ITA Monica

Montecarlo Vin Sinto TUSCANY, ITA Trebbiano Toscano 40-60%, Semillion, Pinot Grigio, Pinot Bianco, Vermentino, Sauvignon Blanc and/or Roussanne 40-60%, (other local white varieties 20% max)

Montecompatri Colonna LATIUM, ITA Malvasia di Candia and/or Puntinata 70% max, Trebbiano Toscano, Trebbiano Verde and/or Trebbiano Giallo 30%, (*Bellone* and/or *Bonvino* 10% max)

Monteregio di Massa Marittima Vin Santo TUSCANY, ITA Trebbiano Toscano and/or Malvasia 70% min, other local white varieties 30% max

Monteregio di Massa Marittima Vin Santo Occhio di Pernice
TUSCANY, ITA Sangiovese 50-70%, Malvasia Nera 10-50%, other local red varieties 30% max

Montescudaio Vin Santo TUSCANY, ITA Trebbiano Toscano 50% min, other local white varieties 50% max

Moscadello di Montalcino TUSCANY, ITA Moscato 85% min (other local white varieties 15% max)

Moscatel de Setúbal PORTUGAL **white:** *Moscatel Graúdo* 67% min, other local varieties 33% max **red:** *Moscatel Galego Roxo* 67% min, other local varieties 33% max

Moscato di Cagliari SARDINIA, ITA Moscato

Moscato di Noto SICILY, ITA Moscato

Moscato di Pantelleria SICILY, ITA Zibibbo

Moscato di Scanzo LOMBARDY, ITA *Moscato di Scanzo*

Moscato di Siracusa SICILY, ITA Moscato

Moscato di Sorso Sennori SARDINIA, ITA Moscato

Moscato di Trani APULIA, ITA Moscato 85% min, (other local white varieties 15% max)

Moscato Passito di Pantelleria SICILY, ITA Zibibbo 95% min (other local white varieties 5% max)

Muscat du Cap Corse CORSICA, FRA Muscat Blanc

Muscat de Frontignan LANGUEDOC-ROUSSILLON, FRA Muscat Blanc

Muscat de Lunel LANGUEDOC-ROUSSILLON, FRA Muscat Blanc

Muscat de Rivesaltes LANGUEDOC-ROUSSILLON, FRA Muscat Blanc, Muscat d'Alexandrie

Muscat de St.-Jean-de-Minervois LANGUEDOC-ROUSSILLON, FRA Muscat Blanc

Muscat of Cephalonia / Kefalonía GREECE Muscat Blanc

Muscat of Lemnos / Límnos GREECE Muscat d'Alexandrie

Muscat of Patras / Pátra GREECE Muscat Blanc

Muscat of Rhodes GREECE Muscat Blanc

Muscat of Samos GREECE Muscat Blanc

Muscat Rion of Patras / Rio of Pátra GREECE Muscat Blanc

Nasco di Cagliari SARDINIA, ITA *Nasco*

Offida Passerina Passito MARCHES, ITA *Passerina* 85% (other local non-aromatic white varieties 15% max)

Oltrepo Pavese LOMBARDY, ITA The following varietals: Bonarda, Malvasia, Moscato

Orcia Vin Santo TUSCANY, ITA Trebbiano Toscano 50%, other local white varieties 50% max

Orvieto UMBRIA & LATIUM, ITA Trebbiano Toscano 40-60%, Verdello 15-25%, (Grechetto, Canaiolo and/or Malvasia Toscana 20%, other local white varieties 15% max)

Pagadebit di Romagna EMILIA-ROMAGNA, ITA Bombino Bianco 85%, other local white varieties 15% max

Pale Cream Sherry SPAIN Palomino, (Pedro Ximénez, Moscatel)

Palmela Licoroso PORTUGAL Castelão 67% min, Alfrocheiro, *Bastardo*, Cabernet Sauvignon and/or Trincadeira 33% max

Pico PORTUGAL Verdelho, Arinto, *Terrantez*

Piemonte Moscato PIEDMONT, ITA Moscato

Port PORTUGAL Touriga National, Tinta Barroca, Tinto Cão, Tempranillo, Touriga Franca, Tinta Amarela

Premières Côtes de Bordeaux BORDEAUX, FRA Sémillon, Sauvignon Blanc, (Muscadelle)

Primitivo di Manduria PUGLIA, ITA Primitivo

Quarts-de-Chaume LOIRE, FRA Chenin Blanc

Ramandolo FRIULI-VENEZIA GIULIA, ITA *Verduzzo*

Rasteau RHÔNE, FRA *Grenache Gris* or Grenache Blanc 90% min, (Syrah, Mourvèdre, Cinsaut, *Terret Noir*, Counoise, Picpoul, Muscardin, *Picardin*, *Vaccarèse*, Clairette, Roussanne, Bourboulenc, Marsanne, Viognier, Carignan, Pinot Blanc, Mauzac, *Pascal Blanc*, Ugni Blanc, *Calitor*, Gamay, *Camarèse*)

Rasteau Rancio RHÔNE, FRA *Grenache Gris* or Grenache Blanc 90% min, (Syrah, Mourvèdre, Cinsaut, *Terret Noir*, Counoise, Picpoul, Muscardin, *Picardin*, *Vaccarèse*, Clairette, Roussanne, Bourboulenc, Marsanne, Viognier, Carignan, Pinot Blanc, Mauzac, *Pascal Blanc*, Ugni Blanc, *Calitor*, Gamay, *Camarèse*)

Recioto della Valpolicella VENETO, ITA Corvina 40%-70%, Rondinella 20-40%, Molinara 5-25%, (Barbera, *Negrara Trentina*, *Rossignola*, Sangiovese)

Recioto di Soave VENETO, ITA Garganega 70% min, (Pinot Bianco, Chardonnay, Trebbiano)

Rivesaltes LANGUEDOC-ROUSSILLON, FRA Muscat Blanc, Muscat d'Alexandrie, Grenache, *Grenache Gris*, Grenache Blanc, Macabéo, *Tourbat*, (Carignan, Cinsault, Syrah, Palamino)

Rosette SOUTHWEST, FRA Sémillon, Sauvignon Blanc, Muscadelle

Ste-Croix-du-Mont BORDEAUX, FRA Sémillon, Sauvignon Blanc, (Muscadelle)

San Martino della Battaglia LOMBARDY/VENETO, ITA Tocai Friulano 80%, (other local white varieties 20% max)

Sant'Antimo Vin Santo TUSCANY, ITA Trebbiano Toscano and/or Malvasia Bianca 70% min, other local white varieties 30% max

Sant'Antimo Vin Santo Occio di Pernice TUSCANY, ITA Sangiovese 50-70%, Malvasia Nera 30-50% (other local red varieties 20% max)

Santorini GREECE Assyrtiko, (*Aidáni Aspro, Athíiri*)

Sardegna Semidano SARDINIA, ITA *Semidano* 85% (other local white varieties 15% max)

Saussignac SOUTHWEST, FRA Sémillon, Sauvignon Blanc, Muscadelle, Chenin Blanc

Sauternes BORDEAUX Sémillon, Sauvignon Blanc, (Muscadelle)

> **Château d'Yquem**, the most famous Sauternes, has vineyards comprising 80% Sémillon, and 20% Sauvignon Blanc

Sitía GREECE *Liátiko* 80%, (*Mandilariá* 20%)

Tokaji Aszú HUNGARY Furmint, Hársevelü, (Muscat Blanc, *Orémus*)

Tokaji Aszú Essencia HUNGARY Furmint, Hársevelü, (Muscat Blanc, *Orémus*)

DESSERT WINES

Tokaji Szamorodni HUNGARY Furmint, Hársevelü, (Muscat Blanc, *Orémus*)

Trentino Vin Santo TRENTINO-ALTO ADIGE, ITA *Nosiola* 85-100%, (other local non-aromatic varieties 15% max)

Val d'Arbia Vin Santo TUSCANY, ITA Trebbiano Toscano and/or Malvasia del Chianti 70-90%, Chardonnay 10-30%

Val di Cornia Aleatico Passito TUSCANY, ITA Aleatico

Val di Cornia Ansonica Passito TUSCANY, ITA Ansonica

Valcalepio Moscato Passito LOMBARDY, ITA Moscato di Scanzo

Valdichiana Vin Santo TUSCANY, ITA Trebbiano Toscano and/or Malvasia Bianca 50%, other local non-aromatic white varieties 50% max

Valencia SPAIN Moscatel de Alejandría

Valle d'Aosta Chambave Moscato AOSTA, ITA Moscato

Valle d'Aosta Nus Malvoisie Passito AOSTA, ITA Pinot Grigio

Vernaccia di Oristano SARDINIA, ITA Vernaccia di Oristano

Vicenza VENETO, ITA Garganega 50%, other local non-aromatic white varieties 50%. The following varietal wine is also made: Moscato

Vin Santo del Chianti TUSCANY, ITA Trebbiano Toscano and/or Malvasia 70%, other local varieties 30% max

Vin Santo del Chianti Classico TUSCANY, ITA Trebbiano Toscano and/or Malvasia 70%, other local varieties 30% max

Vin Santo di Montepulciano TUSCANY, ITA Malvasia Bianca, Grechetto, and/or Trebbiano Toscano 70%, other local white varieties 30% max

Vin Santo Occhio di Pernice del Chianti TUSCANY, ITA Sangiovese 50%, other local varieties 50% max

Vin Santo Occhio di Pernice del Chianti Classico TUSCANY, ITA Sangiovese 50%, other local varieties 50% max

Vin Santo Occhio di Pernice di Montepulciano TUSCANY, ITA Sangiovese 50%, other local varieties 50% max

DESSERT WINES

BIBLIOGRAPHY

Our research was both through our personal tastings and the following resources. The table wouldn't have been possible to the extensive groundwork laid by them. We are especially indebted to the work of Pierre Galet, Jancis Robinson and Anthony J. Hawkins.

Anderson, Burton *Italian Wines* (2004, New York: The Italian Trade Commission) http://www.italianmade.com/wines/home.cfm

Belfrage, Nicolas *Brunello to Zibibbo; The Wines of Tuscany, Central and Southern Italy* (London: Faber and Faber, 1999)

Bastianich, Joseph & David Lynch *Vino Italiano The Regional Wines of Italy* (New York: Clarkson Potter/Publishers, 2002)

Bird, David *Understanding Wine Technology: The Science of Wine Explained* (Notinghamshire, UK: DBQA Publishing, 2000)

Cass, Bruce & Jancis Robinson *The Oxford Comanion to the Wines of North America* (Oxford: Oxford University Press, 2000)

Cobb, Nick & Christina Cobb *Greek Winegrape Varieties* (2004) http://www.greekwinemakers.com/czone/varieties/varieties.shtml

Clark, Oz & Margaret Rand *Oz Clarke's Encyclopedia of Grapes* (London: Websters International Publishers, 2001)

Federal Centre for Breeding Research on Cultivated Plants (BAZ) & Institute for Grapevine Breeding (Geilweilerhof) *European Vitis Database* (2002, The German Centre for Documentation and Information in Agriculture (ZADI)) http://www.genres.de/eccdb/vitis/

Federal Centre for Breeding Research on Cultivated Plants (BAZ) & Institute for Grapevine Breeding (Geilweilerhof) *Vitis International Variety Catalogue* (1999, The German Centre for Documentation and Information in Agriculture (ZADI)) http://www.genres.de/idb/vitis/vitis.htm

Foulkes, Christopher et al *Larousse Encyclopedia of Wine*, 2nd Ed. (Paris: Larousse/VUEF, 2001)

Galet, Pierre *Dictionnaire Encyclopédique des Cépages* (Hachette Livre, 2000)

Galet, Pierre *Grape Varieties* (English Translation: Cassell Illustrated, London, 2002; Hachette Livre, 2001)

Garr, Robin *Wine Lover's Page* (1981-2004) http://www.wine-lovers-page.com/

Hawkins, Anthony J. *THE SUPER GIGANTIC Y2K WINEGRAPE GLOSSARY* (2004) http://www.stratsplace.com/hawkins/wgg.html

Herbst, Ron & Sharon Tyler Herbst *Wine Lover's Companion* (Barron's Educational Series, Inc., Hauppauge, New York, 1995)

Instituto da Vinha e do Vinho *Denominações de Origem* (2004, Instituto da Vinha e do Vinho, Ministério da Agricultura, Desenvolvimento Rural e Pescas, Portugal) http://www.ivv.min-agricultura.pt/vinhos

Jackson, Ronald S. *Wine Tasting: A Professional Handbook* (London: Academic Press, 2002)

Jeffs, Julian *The Wines of Spain* (London: Faber and Faber, 1999)

Johnson, Hugh & Jancis Robinson *The World Atlas of Wine* (London: Mitchell Beazley, 2001)

Kolpan, Steven, Brian H. Smith & Michael A. Weiss *Exploring Wine, 2nd Edition* (New York: John Wiley & Sons, 2002)

LaMar, Jim et al. *Wine Grape and Varietal Profiles* (1999-2004, Professional Friends of Wine) http://www.winepros.org/wine101/grape_profiles/varietals.htm

Liddell, Alex *The Wines of Hungary* (London: Mitchell Beazley, 2003)

Mayson, Richard *The Wines and Vineyards of Portugal* (London: Mitchell Beazley, 2003)

Peynaud, Emile *The Taste of Wine* trans. Michael Schuster (London: Macdonald & Co., 1987)

Robinson, Jancis *Jancis Robinson's Guide to Wine Grapes* (Oxford: Oxford University Press, 1996)

Robinson, Jancis Ed. *The Oxford Companion to Wine*, 2nd Ed. (Oxford: Oxford University Press, 1999)

Stevenson, Tom Ed. *The New Sotheby's Wine Encyclopedia* (London: Dorling Kindersley, 1997)

Sutcliffe, Serena Ed. *Great Vineyards and Winemakers* (London: Macdonald & Co., 1981)

Zraly, Kevin *Windows on the World Complete Wine Course* (New York: Sterling Publishing, 2001)